Homer

P.

S. M. A. R.

AM I ALIVE?

A Surviving Flight Attendant's Struggle and Inspiring Triumph over Tragedy

Sandy Purl
with Gregg Lewis

1817

Harper & Row, Publishers, San Francisco

Cambridge, Hagerstown, New York, Philadelphia
London, Mexico City, São Paulo, Singapore, Sydney

This book accurately portrays Sandy Purl Ward's experiences surrounding the crash of Southern Airways flight 242. The names used in this book are not real names and identifying details have been changed with the exception of members of the Purl family, the air crew and passengers of flight 242, the people of New Hope, Georgia, survivors of other airline crashes, Dr. Joseph Peek, Ken Carrolin, Scott Newell, Carla Harris, Mary Michaluk, Shannon Nocera-Campbell, Del Mott, and Margaret Barbeau.

FIRST EDITION

Library of Congress Cataloging in Publication Data

Purl, Sandy.
  Am I alive?

  1. Survival (after airplane accidents, shipwrecks, etc.) 2. Purl, Sandy.
3. Air lines—United States—Flight attendants—Biography. I. Lewis, Gregg A.
II. Title.
TL553.7.P87 1986   363.1'24'0924 [B]   85–45364
ISBN 0-06-250691-9

---

86 87 88 89 90 RRD 10 9 8 7 6 5 4 3 2 1

Acknowledgments

So many wonderful people deserve and have my gratitude. But I'm able to name only a few of them here as I offer special thanks:

To my twin, Candy, and the rest of my family for overwhelming me with unconditional love;

To many friends, such as Kitty and Carl Seabolt and Lindy Johnson, who played big parts in my story, if not in the book;

To the employees and management of Republic Airlines for their flexibility, their affirmation, and a new start;

To Dr. Joseph Peek for his professional care and his personal caring;

To Charlie and Mildred Newman and the other people of New Hope for compassion and friendship offered to me in the face of their own loss;

To Del Mott and others in the airline industry who've given a voice to survivors and then responded to our needs;

To Suzanne Balzer, Judy Kessler, and other supportive union friends in the AFA;

And most of all to my loving husband, Bob McAfee, whose unfailing patience, strength, and support have enabled me to bring this story to a conclusion and begin the rest of my life.

To the memory of Captain William McKenzie, First Officer Lyman Keele, and the others who died in the crash of Southern Flight 242,

To all the victims of airline disasters before and since,

To Cathy Lemoine and all my fellow survivors.

Chapter 1

The jangling phone rudely ended the short night between flights. I hurriedly curled my long auburn hair, put some blush and mascara on my face, and slipped into my crisply ironed uniform. For a moment, I looked into the mirror—a moment's gathering myself together before embarking on a new day, a rushed work schedule. I was twenty-four years old; my reflection was young and attractive. All systems go! I grabbed my flight bag and raced down the hotel stairs to check out.

A few minutes later, the rest of the Southern Airways flight crew joined me as we squeezed into a cab for the dreary, slow ride from the motel to the Muscle Shoals airport. The rhythmic swish-swish-swish of the windshield wipers prophesied yet another gloomy, turbulent day of flying across the Southeast. We had thirteen stops ahead of us.

I decided to focus on getting home to New Orleans and my husband, Mike. He'd hinted at special plans he had made for that evening. I hoped the day would go by fast.

I never once dreamed of being a flight attendant as I grew up. Yet I doubt any family could have been any better than mine as a preparation for my eventual career. The youngest of eight children, and a twin, I spent my childhood learning to live with and relate to a variety of people. My father's Air Force career kept us moving around the United States. So meeting new people became an accomplished skill, transience seemed a way of life, and travel always meant new adventures and experiences.

Because my father was a firefighter in the service and my mother was a military nurse, our family was always very safety conscious. As far back as I remember, we held family fire drills and I was taught what to do in any emergency.

The most significant family event so far had been father's two-year battle (in vain) against cancer. The diagnosis and the removal of the first tumor came the summer before my junior year of high school. But neither the subsequent operations nor his slow, steady deterioration felt real to me. He couldn't be dying—he was my father!

And in fact he worked as long as he could and kept his spirits high. He never lost his dry sense of humor, never stopped teasing his kids. He took obvious pride in our accomplishments. Looking back, I see that much of my motivation for achievement in high school came from my father; I wanted to make him proud.

In February of my senior year I won the "Girl Student of the Year" award in the distributive education (a work study) program at Jonesboro (Georgia) High School that allowed me to go to school half days and work the rest for local employers. My father had planned to go with me to the district competition, but he wasn't feeling very well when the day came. So he stayed home, and I went without him.

At five o'clock that afternoon, I rushed down our driveway only to see an ambulance parked by our front door. The paramedics already had him on a stretcher; he was protesting, "Nope, no way! I won't go until my girl gets back!" Then I saw his eyes light up as he caught sight of me. Swallowing my tears, I told him I'd won this round and would be going to the state finals. "Honey," he said, "I'm just so proud of you!" But he winced as he spoke, and I was shocked to see how deathly pale he was. I stepped aside as the paramedics wheeled him out the walk and loaded him into the ambulance. I stood frozen in our bare, wintry yard watching the flashing lights and listening to the siren howling as they took him away. For the first time I recognized clearly that my father might die.

On March 23, 1971, I was with my father, and my sister Sue, in his hospital room. He remained conscious, never complaining of the pain. We'd talked about some of my plans for the coming weeks, and he'd told me he wanted me to go on with my schedule.

I could hear the pain make his voice ragged when he whispered, "Come here, Babe." That was his nickname for me.

I bent toward him and asked, "What do you want, Daddy?"

"Hold me," he replied softly. "Hold me tight."

So I took him in my arms, just as a nurse entered the room. "Don't move," she said kindly. "I've got to get some of the fluid out of your chest," she explained to my father. "Your daughter can help by holding you."

She stepped to the side of his bed, and inserted a giant needle into his chest cavity. I felt him flinch with the pain as she extracted a syringe full of fluid from around his lungs. His breath became noticeably more labored and the nurse turned to my sister to say, "Call your mother." Sue hurried into the hall to get her.

As I held my father, I looked into his eyes, saw his pain and said, "Go ahead, Daddy. I know you're hurting." With that permission, he let go. I felt the life seep out of his body as my mother burst into the room crying, "Don't go, Tom! Don't go!"

But he was already gone.

I didn't realize it then, but I was deeply traumatized, wounded, by that experience with my father. (At least in my own mind, I was implicated in his death.) By the time his funeral was over, I had vowed to myself I would never look at another dead body as long as I lived.

In the two months after his death, I went through the motions of senior year in high school. I was elected "Best Personality" by my fellow members of the class of 1971. In June my twin sister, Candy, and I, plus my sister Sue, who is only ten months older than we are, graduated from high school. But accomplishments seemed hollow without my father to share them. I was a daddy's girl without a daddy.

Right after graduation I took a traveling job, training photographers for the baby photography company I'd worked part-time for during high school; my territory covered Nebraska, Wyoming, and Colorado. Driving those long, empty stretches of western interstates, I found myself alone, really alone, for the first time. It scared me. But it also gave me time to think. I decided that what I really wanted to do with my life was help other people.

So I quit my job to attend a local community college near home with plans to go into nursing. But even before my first term was up, I realized that college expenses were quickly depleting my savings. Too independent to consider applying for government loans, I pondered other money-making possibilities.

That's why I entered the Miss Clayton County and Miss South Cobb County beauty pageants; I knew the winners would take home a large scholarship check. I was voted Miss Congeniality in both contests. But there was no monetary prize attached to those honors, so I went home disappointed. Since I couldn't pay tuition with trophies, I had to come up with the money some other way.

Right in the middle of an English test at the end of my fall quarter, my instructor dropped a page of classified ads on my desk. She pointed to an item she had marked: "Flight Attendants Wanted." Southern Airways was taking applications that very day at their local office.

I'd confided in her about my financial situation and my growing uncertainty about continuing school. When I turned in my test, she told me, "I think you ought to consider applying for one of those positions with Southern. You could earn some money and buy some time to decide about your future."

I went straight from school to the Southern Airways office. The moment I walked into the waiting room and looked around, I told myself, *"It's hopeless, girl."* The crowd of girls looked like they were putting on another beauty pageant!

Ordinarily I liked my looks. I had 5 feet 4 inches of trim figure. I'd had my auburn hair blunt-cut into a short "page boy." My best feature, big brown eyes, are accented by long black lashes. A light sprinkle of freckles dust my nose, cheeks, and forehead.

But surveying that waiting room, I felt all my usual confidence fading faster than a pair of jeans in Clorox.

Every girl in the place was dressed fit to kill. And there I stood in my school clothes with hardly any makeup. A light afternoon rain had left my hair straight. I felt like turning and walking out, but instead I rallied my best Miss Congeniality smile and greeted the whole room. Not one person responded. So I took an application and sat down to fill it out. "I've got nothing to lose," I told myself.

An hour or so later a secretary directed me into an adjacent office for a short interview. A man asked me a few questions about things I'd written on the application. He was particularly interested in knowing how and why I'd learned sign language.

I explained that when I'd run for office in my high school Tri-Hi-Y Club, one of the schools in the district had been the Georgia School for the Deaf. I'd learned Sign so I could communicate with those kids. Before long I'd taught my whole family Sign, and I'd invite my deaf friends over to our house for weekends and holidays.

When the interview concluded, the man told me I'd hear from Southern one way or the other within a few days. I headed home without high expectations.

When I finally called Southern a week later, I could hear the woman on the other end of the phone shuffling papers before she said, "Congratulations, Sandy. You start training on January 2!" So I spent the Christmas season anticipating a new stage in life.

Training school was fun. I've always enjoyed making new friends; and being housed all together in a local motel made it feel as if we were part of some long convention. But there was work too. Classes lasted from morning till night. And there was more studying to be done than I'd expected. By the time we'd finished the first week in training, I was realizing there was much more to being an airline flight attendant than the stereotyped, "Coffee, tea or me" image.

My most memorable training experience occurred during the last week, when we covered emergency procedures. After the lecturer had discussed and demonstrated oxygen supplies, window exits, inflatable chutes, and special flotation equipment, I naively asked, "Where are the parachutes kept?"

The whole class broke into laughter, thinking, "That's Sandy, cutting up again!" But I wasn't joking; when I imagined an airborne emergency, I pictured a plane catching fire in the sky and everyone bailing out. When the laughter died down and the instructor went on, I interrupted again, "Really. Where *are* the parachutes?"

This time the laughter was different, as everyone realized I was serious. The instructor, obviously embarrassed for me, quickly explained that commercial airline flights carried no parachutes.

I was teased about that incident for years. I think every new class of flight attendants heard the story.

But my naiveté didn't keep me from graduating in good standing on January 26, 1973. And I think, because of having to consciously reconsider the possible implications of an aircraft emergency, I began flying that next month with a growing understanding of the seriousness of my responsibility as a flight attendant.

Within three months, in April 1973, I was called on to respond in a real life-or-death situation. We were greeting passengers on a flight out of Mobile, Alabama, when two local policemen strode down the aisle, holding, on either side, an eighteen-year-old girl who looked down at the floor even as I said, "Hello." Tears rolled one by one down her chalk-white face; she shook her long hair forward over her cheeks, clearly to win a little privacy for herself. She was covered with ugly, discolored bruises and angry-looking cuts. But all the policemen would say was that she had to go to Memphis for medical treatment. I helped seat her, and put her bag and coat in the overhead storage compartment. Later, as soon as the "No Smoking" light went off, I got out of my jumpseat and went to see if I could make her more comfortable.

I was reaching over to recline her seat when I noticed the gray tint of her lips. She wasn't breathing! I unbuckled her and slung her sideways across the seat in a single motion. Immediately I dropped down beside her and started mouth-to-mouth resuscitation.

But something broke open inside me; instead of an eighteen-year-old girl, I saw a fifty-year-old man in a hospital bed. Each time I paused for breath, I whispered, "Don't die on me, Daddy! *Please* don't die!"

Within moments the other flight attendant was standing over me asking, "What did you say, Sandy? Can I do something?" I didn't respond. I just continued the mouth-to-mouth rhythm, moaning, "Don't die, Daddy! *Please* don't die!" After a few minutes, we tried to adminster our emergency oxygen to the girl, but it wasn't enough. So I resumed mouth-to-mouth while the plane made an emergency landing in Gulfport/Biloxi, where an ambulance met us.

We learned later that the girl had been raped and beaten the night before. And she'd taken an overdose of the medicine that had been prescribed for her by a doctor in Mobile. The mouth-to-mouth work had given her the chance she needed to live, and I received a commendation for my actions. But for me the biggest significance in the episode was realizing that I had not truly accepted my father's death.

I didn't deal with it now, either. Instead, I immersed myself in my new career. I could get on a plane and think of nothing but the needs of the people around me. Flying offered new friends, new family. Flying became my life.

It was even because of flying that I met Mike. I'd gone down to Ft. Walton Beach, Florida, to stay with a flight attendant friend on my days off. She arranged a blind date for me with an Air Force pilot she knew, and we went out to a dinner-dance club. I was having a lousy evening, and my blind date wasn't much happier. At one point, when my date excused himself to go to the men's room, this other guy, who looked a lot like a thirty-year-old version of Doc Severinson, walked over and asked me to dance. I said no, explaining that I was there with a date. He said he understood, but he'd like to see me some time. Then he grinned real big and said, "My name is Mike," and handed me a business card. He was gone before my date returned.

Evidently my date wasn't any more interested in me than I was in him, because he had me home by 9:30 P.M. Once he was gone, I headed back to the club to see if I could find this guy "Mike." I did, and we spent the next few hours dancing and getting to know each other. I went home to Atlanta thinking that was the end of that. But Mike sent me flowers for Easter. And the next time I went through Ft. Walton, we had our second date.

I transferred to Southern's Ft. Walton base in June, and one year later I moved in with Mike. I quickly concluded Mike was the perfect guy for me. He had eleven years of age on me, which I saw as a sign of maturity and stability. I saw him as someone who could and would take care of me. Yet he was something of a free spirit, who was well known around Ft. Walton. We had a lot of fun together; he taught me to water ski and he introduced me to deep sea fishing.

Mike might have married me right away, but emotionally I wasn't ready. I couldn't imagine getting married without my father to walk me down the aisle. So while Mike and I naturally spent a lot of time together, we lived our own separate lives. He had his own interests and business acquaintances. And as for me, flying remained my primary world.

In 1975 I was appointed safety representative for our Transportation Workers Union local in Ft. Walton. In that role it was my responsibility to fill out TWU reports on any malfunctioning or missing equipment and to report any violations of safety procedures. I also served on committees with other Southern safety reps, committees that discussed the aftermath of Eastern's recent crashes in Charlotte and the Everglades.

I was sent, with my counterparts from all Southern and Eastern Airlines bases, to attend the Civil Aeromedical Institute (CAMI) in Oklahoma City. There we received out first true-to-life exposure to in-flight emergencies. We practiced evacuations from an actual smoke-filled cabin and used emergency oxygen masks in a decompression chamber. We witnessed experiments to improve crash-survivability rates—seatbelt tolerance tests, and tests for flame-retardant materials for use in cabins and uniforms.

I left our seminar at CAMI impressed with and shaken by the responsibility we had for passenger safety. I became more of a stickler than ever about safety regulations. Every piece of equipment on my flights was double-checked. And if any item of carry-on luggage didn't fit all the way under the seat, it had to be checked, regardless of who brought it on.

The seriousness of my role as flight attendant and the sobering dependence passengers exhibit toward the crew was emphasized for me by a potentially serious airborne emergency that actually turned out to be quite funny. One day during a flight, the cabin door I had been responsible for securing properly somehow came unsealed and the cabin decompressed. Many of the passengers began to experience real physical distress.

I quickly made my way to the public address mike and in my haste to rectify the problem I said, "Those of you who are experiencing discomfort with your ears, hold your ears and blow out. Then put your finger in your nose and wiggle it." But when I peeked around the partition to see how many people were complying with the instructions I saw a whole cabinful of people with fingers up their noses, obediently trying to blow out through their ears. "Oh, gross," I thought, torn between laughter at the ludicrous sight and tears over my bungled instructions. "Ladies and gentlemen," I repeated over the PA, "now hold your *nose* and blow out, then put your *finger* in your *ear* and wiggle it." Without a split-second's hesitation, everyone obeyed, evidently assuming I was giving them Step 2.

Later I laughed about the incident with friends. But it also impressed me once and for all what absolute trust passengers would place in me during any emergency. And I vowed never to take that part of my job lightly.

Mike and I were finally married in February 1976, in the church I'd attended as a teenager in Jonesboro, Georgia. I no longer had a church I could call my own because I'd pretty much abandoned my childhood faith and all its trappings when God failed to answer my prayers to keep my father alive. And I walked into that church on my bridegroom's arm because there was still no one I thought could replace my father.

I'd always expected marriage to be a big turning point in life. But it wasn't, really. I'd thought it would be a partnership, a true blending of two lives becoming one. But that didn't happen either. Mike and I shared a home and a lot of time together. I invested a major effort in trying to be a loving stepmother to his two young boys from an earlier marriage. I quickly came to love his kids, but our lives as husband and wife never seemed to become one. We each had major parts of our lives—especially our friends, our jobs, and our business associates—in which we were practically strangers. As a result, we seldom communicated on the meaningful, emotionally intimate level I wanted.

We did however come to a joint decision to move to New Orleans that September. Soon after I transferred I began to experience nameless anxieties about flying. Finally, in December 1976, fearing that I might not be able to carry out my responsibilities in an emergency, I reported my anxiety problem to the national office in Atlanta and asked for help.

After hearing all my symptoms and reviewing my record (which was good), the head of flight attendant services granted me thirty days medical leave, to seek help. I went to a doctor in New Orleans, who successfully treated me with hypnosis. When I went back to work at the end of my leave, all the anxieties were gone.

Three months later I heard the awful news about two Boeing 747 jets colliding and killing over 500 people in the Canary Islands. Even so, I boarded my next flight without a trace of nervousness.

Eight days later, as our crew headed to the Muscle Shoals airport through the morning rain, my only concern about the prospective turbulence was that it might keep me from getting home to New Orleans in time for dinner with Mike.

Chapter 2

Early on April 4, 1977, a cold front moved into the lower Mississippi River Valley and rumbled eastward like a huge bulldozer, shoving a mass of warm, moist air ahead of it. By afternoon, as the front rolled over northern Alabama and on into Georgia, the mixture of warm and cold air created towering clouds in a blackening sky.

Inside one of these giant cumulus clouds, rain started to fall. But before the moisture could reach the ground, it was caught in a violent updraft that channeled it more than five miles back up into the cold air. The rain froze and fell again. This process repeated itself again and again until the interior of this cloud became a vicious maelstrom of hailstones.

I rebuckled my seatbelt as Southern Flight 242 began a bumpy descent into Huntsville, Alabama. Since the beginning of our early morning shift, our crew had flown in and out of Atlanta all day on short hops. Cathy, the other flight attendant, and I had spent nearly all our air time strapped in our jumpseats because of rough skies.

Cathy, a 5-foot, 3-inch blonde, was my senior by eight months. We'd flown together a number of times. So we knew each other's preferences and could work together efficiently and well.

The cockpit crew was just about my favorite. The captain, Bill, always treated flight attendants as fellow professionals with an important role on the airplane. Apart from the professional respect I had for him, he was also a friend.

The first officer, Lyman, was a handsome, dark-haired, former Navy pilot, twenty years younger than the captain. His fun-loving appeal made him enjoyable company. He loved telling stories and jokes—in fact, at one of our stops just the day before he had had all the rest of the crew in stitches, laughing. Lyman said he'd applied as a pilot with another airline and the interviewer, wanting to test his response to an emergency situation, asked him what he'd do if he saw two trains running full speed on the same track and heading right at each other. Lyman said he thought for a moment and said, "Well, I guess I'd say a quick prayer to God and then run get my brother." The man said he certainly understood the prayer part, but he wondered why Lyman would run to get his brother. At this point in telling the story, Lyman had paused and looked around at each of us who were listening. Then he said, "I told the man, 'I knew God could stop it. But if He was busy, I knew my brother had never seen a train wreck.' "

Flying always seemed a lot easier when I worked with people I liked. And on a two-day stint of stormy up-and-down short trips, a compatible crew like ours made the tension and fatigue more bearable. We now only had two more stops to make and our exhausting thirteen-leg assignment would be over.

On the ground in Huntsville, Cathy stationed herself at the door to board and welcome new passengers while I prepared the cabin. My head count of sixty Huntsville boarders, with the twenty-one already on board, gave us a total of eighty-one passengers for the flight back to Atlanta. I was assigned to the rear of the aircraft, and quickly checked to see that all baggage was stowed, seatbelts fastened, and tray tables up. No sooner had I finished my inspection than we began a short taxi—so short that Cathy and I hardly had time to demonstrate the safety instructions before taking our own seats for takeoff.

The plane quickly climbed through the nasty weather—and then descended a couple of thousand feet. I assumed that the cockpit crew was checking radar and talking with ground control to find a smoother course through the storm.

Suddenly the whole sky broke loose. Hail that sounded like a million boulders battered the metal roof. Every passenger in the plane turned in unison and looked at me. The wave of raw emotions on their fearful faces seemed to push me back into my seat. I fought to keep the calm on my face.

Then, above the clattering din, I heard three explosions—Pow! Pow! Pow!—in the left engine. The cabin lights flickered, and the emergency lights kicked on for 15–20 seconds before power was restored in the cabin. But the familiar droning of the left jet was gone. I wondered if the engine had ripped away from the plane.

A few moments later, the hail stopped. I picked up the PA mike again. My own calmness surprised me as I reassured the passengers: "Keep your seatbelts on and securely fastened. There's nothing to be alarmed about. Relax, we should be out of the storm shortly—"

The lights flickered and went out again. When the power returned, I went on with the instructions I'd been drilled to give. "Please check to see that all carry-on baggage is stowed completely under the seat in front of you. In the unlikely event that there is a need for an emergency landing, we do ask that you please grab your ankles. If I scream instructions from the rear of the aircraft, there is nothing to be alarmed about. But in the event there is an emergency and you do hear us holler, please grab your ankles. Thank you for your cooperation and just relax. These are precautionary measures only."

As I finished my announcement, I strained to hear the sound of the right engine. I could hear a steady hum, but it didn't seem normal either. My ears had popped about the time the left engine went and the cabin temperature was quickly rising, so I knew we'd decompressed. Then I smelled smoke—like something electrical burning—I pictured the plane exploding in mid-air and scattering us over the north Georgia countryside.

In the cockpit, First Officer Lyman Keele piloted the crippled DC-9 while Captain William McKenzie raised Atlanta Center on the radio. "Okay, Flight 242 here. We just got our windshield busted, and we'll try to get back up to 15,000 feet. We're at 14,000," McKenzie reported. After checking the top set of gauges on the center console, he added, "Our left engine just cut out."

Less than 30 seconds passed. Suddenly Keele exclaimed, "My God, the other engine's going too"—

"Got the other engine going, too," the captain relayed to Atlanta.

"Southern 242, say again?" the ground controller asked.

"Stand by!" barked McKenzie. "We lost both engines!"

During the next five and a half minutes, the pilots tried desperately to restart the dead engines. Keele reset his course for Dobbins Air Force Base in Marietta. But the field was twenty miles away, and Flight 242 was losing altitude rapidly.

The instant I smelled fire, I knew we were in real trouble. But my first reaction was irritation: "Why today?" I thought. "I'm too busy today. Just one more leg after this, and I could be home! Mike's made special dinner plans."

But such thoughts quickly faded as the seriousness of the situation sank in. Any second I expected an emergency signal from the cockpit. It didn't come, so I finally acted on my own. I unbuckled my seatbelt, stood, and quickly made my way forward to Row 11. Trying to control my voice as much as possible, I reassured everyone that there was nothing to be alarmed about—storm situations such as the one we were experiencing simply called for an emergency briefing.

"This is standard procedure," I said, as calmly and convincingly as I could. "But I want you to listen carefully to all my instructions." I sat on the seat backs of Row 10. Stretching my legs to put my feet on the opposite aisle seat, I demonstrated the brace position for landing—hands on ankles, head between my knees. I individually briefed the people sitting at the window exits, showing them where to pull and how to lift the windows out, and making each one repeat my instructions so I knew he understood. I also told them they were to slide down the trailing edge of the wing and wait to help the passengers following. Everyone was to run 50 yards upwind of the plane. Then I told all the passengers to take off their shoes and stow their eyeglasses in the seat pocket in front of them.

Aware that Cathy had started briefing passengers in the front, I hurried to the rear, to show the passengers in the last seats, Row 20, their escape route. Asking them to get out their briefing cards, I showed how to open the rear bulkhead door, jettison the tail cone, and inflate the tail-cone slide. My jumpseat was the closest to the rear exit, but I didn't think I'd survive impact. I would be strapped into my seat between the engines, and if they didn't explode I was certain to be knocked out or have both legs broken when my jumpseat collapsed.

"If I'm incapacitated," I told the man in Seat 20B, "Your job will be to drag my body out of the way and get to the door as quickly as possible. You won't have time to mess with me, so just pull my body over behind these seats and get out."

He nodded obediently. In fact, every passenger on board the plane responded unquestioningly to my every order without panic, as if I was some sort of goddess. I couldn't believe their calm.

As I returned to my jumpseat, three chimes sounded over the PA system. I quickly picked up my phone and heard Cathy's voice. "Sandy? They would not talk to me. When I looked in, the whole front windshield was cracked."

She paused for a response, but I didn't say anything. My mind raced over the possible implications of Cathy's report, none of them good. She jolted me out of those thoughts when she asked, "Okay, so what do we do?"

I still expected some instruction from the flight crew. "Have they said anything?"

"The captain screamed at me to sit down when I opened the door," Cathy said. "So I didn't ask him a thing. I don't know the results or anything. But I'm sure we're decompressed."

"Yes," I told her. "And we lost an engine." Then I asked her to make sure she had briefed the passengers up front and I reminded her to stow her shoes in a galley compartment.

"I took off my stockings so I wouldn't be sliding," I added.

"That's a good idea," she responded. "Thank you, bye-bye."

The intercom clicked off. I could only wait and wonder what was happening.

While Sandy and Cathy could only speculate on the danger, the cockpit crew knew all too well what was happening. Captain McKenzie eyed the plummeting altimeter and asked Ground Control if there was any airport closer than Dobbins. The first reply was negative.

"I doubt we're going to make it," McKenzie warned. "But we're trying everything to get something started."

"Roger," Ground Control answered. "Well, there is Cartersvile. You're ten miles south of Cartersville, fifteen miles west of Dobbins."

"We'll have to go up there," Keele told the captain.

"Can you give us a vector to Cartersville?" McKenzie asked the ground.

"All right," came the instructions. "Turn left, heading of three-six-zero, direct vector to Cartersville."

Captain McKenzie requested the runway's heading and length. Ground Control asked him to stand by.

Ten seconds passed before Keele said, "Bill, you've got to find me a highway."

McKenzie spotted a blacktopped road.

"Is it straight?" Keele asked, as he checked his gauges and readied his controls for landing.

"No."

"We'll have to take it," Keele said. There was no longer any choice.

The ground controller finally came back to report on the runway: "At Cartersville, three-six-zero, running north and south, the elevation is 756 and uh . . . trying to get the length now . . . it's 3,200 feet long."

"We're putting it on the highway," the captain informed the ground. "We're down to nothing."

Keele called, "Flaps."

"There at 50."

"I hope I can do it, Bill."

"I've got it. I got it!" Keele exclaimed. "I'm going to land right over that guy."

"There's a car ahead," the captain warned.

"I got it, Bill. I've got it now! I got it!"

"Okay. Don't stall it!"

"I gotta bug . . . We're going to do it right here!"

I knew we were low. But thinking we were descending into the Atlanta airport, I kept expecting to hear the five-bell emergency landing signal at any moment. When I noticed a male passenger get up and move to an aisle seat nearer the back, I ran forward and shouted, "Sit down. Now!" I returned to my seat and was standing, leaning forward to put my glasses in a pocket on the last row of seats when I glimpsed tree trunks out the window to my left. Still assuming we were landing on a runway, I started screaming, "Bend down and grab your ankles!"

Just before touchdown, I watched all the passengers go into the brace position. I wasn't yet buckled in my jumpseat on first impact. But when we bounced back up in the air, I yanked the belt across my hips and clamped it shut.

On second impact, a ball of flames flashed through the cabin. I saw one of my passengers catch fire at the same instant I was thrown forward into the brace position. I heard a woman scream. Then the whole world disintegrated around me. Flying bits of debris filled the cabin. I felt as if I were strapped into a big cardboard box rolling down stairs. My arms and legs flailed in front of my face as I tumbled over and over and over. Through it all I kept screaming, "Stay down! Grab your ankles. Grab your ankles . . . "

First Officer Keele had set the plane down right in the middle of Georgia Highway Spur 92—after bouncing once to avoid a car. The right wing had clipped a utility pole at an Amoco station. The left wing almost simultaneously wiped out the power and telephone lines to the New Hope, Georgia, fire station across the street. Careening on down the road, the DC-9's left wing smashed into gas pumps and a car parked in front of Newman's Grocery Store. The massive plane veered sideways and began to shatter and roll, tumbling past a number of homes in the tiny town of New Hope, before coming to rest in a cluster of pine trees off to the side of the road.

Suddenly everything stopped. Now the only sound invading the stillness was the crackling of flames spanning floor to ceiling in front of my jumpseat. For a second I wondered why I hadn't heard the emergency bells. But as my mind began to clear, I realized: "This is the real thing—a real emergency!"

With the wall of fire in front of me, I had only one way to go. I quickly unbuckled my seatbelt, stood, stepped back, and tried to force open the rear emergency exit between the bathrooms. But the handle wouldn't budge.

By now the smoke and fumes were searing my lungs. I began to cough and gasp for air. I knew that the toxic fumes were lethal within 30 seconds. I had to get out. But my vision began to go fuzzy. I watched my own hands slowly clawing their way down the emergency door as my body sagged to the floor.

There's no other way to explain what happened next except to say I felt myself slipping away. I slowly left my body through the back of my head and began to drift gently upward. About 10 feet above the floor of the plane, I looked down through the smoke and the flames and saw *my own body*, crumpled at the rear of the burning cabin.

At the same time, from my curled position on the floor, I was *watching* this happen. It was as if my eyes were turned around and looking out the back of my head. I could see myself hovering above the flames, waving goodbye to myself.

From above, looking down, I felt no real emotion until my father appeared beside me and took my hand. Instantly, I was engulfed by an overwhelming sense of peace and calm and a love that hadn't existed in my life since he had died six years before. But as I looked down at my flame-trapped body, fear returned. "I don't want to go back!" I pleaded. but my father gently answered, "It'll be all right, Sandy. You'll be okay."

The next thing I knew I was coughing on the fumes again and screaming out a prayer in my mind, "God! I survived impact— please don't let me die here by myself between these bathrooms."

The moment those words crossed my consciousness, I felt something grip me under the arms and jerk me to my feet. Certain I would die if I stayed where I was, I stepped forward, determined to go through the fire to the first window exit in the cabin. "If I don't make it," I thought, "at least I'll die with my passengers."

But as I shielded my face with an arm and moved forward, the wall of flames parted like a curtain, and I stepped out of the plane onto solid ground.

Chapter 3

I had taken only a half-dozen dazed steps away from the aircraft when an explosion knocked me to the ground. Sputtering and gagging on the dirt in my mouth, I looked back over my shoulder to see the tail section—with my jumpseat between the two bathrooms—completely engulfed in flames. The rear of the cabin had broken away between my seat and the last row of passengers.

Large, twisted pieces of the plane lay scattered around me. The stench of jet fuel, pine smoke, and burning flesh filled the air. Another explosion rocked the tail wreckage. Finally I picked myself up and staggered to the road.

When I reached the pavement, an awkward weight pulled at my shoulders. I looked down to see a burn-blackened body under each arm. Both men were dead. As I laid them down at the edge of the roadway, I tried to remember how they'd gotten there. But I didn't know.

Then I spotted a blue pickup truck racing toward me on the highway. I ran out to the middle of the blacktop and waved my arms. As the truck screeched to a halt, I ran to the driver's door. "A Southern DC-9 just crashed!" I told him. "I'm a stewardess. You've got to help!"

"How many people?" he asked.

My mind went blank. "I don't remember. We were almost full—about a hundred."

The driver didn't wait for anything else. He shifted into gear and raced up the hill. I ran after him, screaming, "Come back! Come back! We need help!"

Finally giving up the chase, I stopped. And for the first time I turned and looked at the holocaust stretching for hundreds of yards along that little country highway.

At the crest of the hill ahead of Sandy, a downed utility pole at the Amoco station marked the spot the plane had first touched down.

Halfway up the slope, on the right, long tongues of fire billowed into the sky from Newman's Grocery, fueled by the gas tanks in front of the small store.

Burning, broken pines and torn metal littered the entire scene. Incredibly, not one of the houses lining the road had been struck by the plane. The largest remains of the aircraft rested in the heavily wooded front yard of the one house built back away from the highway.

A man stumbled away from the biggest piece of wreckage and staggered toward the road. All his clothes had burned off him, except for his underwear and two strips of elastic around his ankles where his socks had been.

"If there's one survivor, maybe there are more." I ran back toward the two biggest sections of the cabin. The ground near the wreckage was covered with charred victims. One moved a leg, so I dragged him out of the wreckage to the road and hurriedly returned to search for anyone else who might still be alive. I checked every body I found for a twitch of the leg or a wiggling of a finger. The slightest movement offered a glimmer of hope.

But even as I dragged another passenger to the edge of the road, I felt so helpless. So alone. "I gotta get help." The thought became an instant obsession. I carefully eased the body I was carrying to the ground, looked around, and headed to the nearest home across the highway.

I heard a woman's voice screaming, "Help that boy. Somebody help that boy!" The lady stood in a nearby driveway and pointed back toward the crash. I turned to see a seat that had rolled free from the cabin. The passenger was still strapped in, and struggling to get out.

But I didn't have time to go back. I had to get to a phone. As I ran up the driveway across the road from the crash, an elderly couple came out to stand terrified on their porch. "Can I use your phone?" I asked. "I have to call for help."

"Sure," the man nodded. But he was looking past me. His wife gasped, and I whirled to see why.

A passenger came half running, half reeling toward us. The back of his suit still smoldered. His arms and face were black with burns. I knocked him to the ground and rolled him in the grass to put out the fire. Ordering the couple to cover him and keep him still, I ran into the house.

I found the phone with no trouble. But when I picked up the receiver I heard no dial tone. Instinctively I reached into my serving smock, pulled a quarter out of my liquor change, and desperately searched the phone for a slot to drop the money in. Seconds passed before I realized the phone was dead. I dropped the receiver and rushed back outside.

Rescue vehicles were beginning to arrive. "Help is coming," I thought. But now I had a new obsession: "I have to call Mike. I have to let him know I'm okay." A man with a service station shirt came running up. He took my arm and tried to lead me away.

"I'm a stewardess." I said, jerking free. "I have to stay. But you can help. You can call my husband and tell him I'm okay. You *have* to call him!"

I grabbed the man's pen and a piece of paper sticking out of his pocket and quickly wrote down my name, Mike's name, and our home number in New Orleans.

"But lady, the phones—"

"Just call him," I ordered as I started back down the road.

While I tried to decide what to do next, I paced along the road, clenching and unclenching my fists, saying out loud, "Stay calm. Stay calm."

My most overpowering thought was that number one fact, drilled into us in training and in all the safety courses I'd had. "You are responsible for your passengers." I had to keep searching for survivors.

I ran back to the largest cabin section of the plane and began moving sheets of hot metal and pulling more bodies out of the wreckage. I shouted instructions at the gathering bystanders— telling them to cover the people still alive and treat them for shock. And I did it all without thinking.

Something had snapped inside me; I was functioning purely on instinct and adrenaline. From the time I'd first reached the road and looked down to see the two corpses under my arms, I'd felt more like a dispassionate observer than a participant. I was an actress, acting out an unbelievable role in a gruesome disaster movie being projected in circle-vision.

Once, as I sifted through the jagged wreckage, I stopped and stared with surprise to see my own bare feet covered with blood from open, oozing cuts. But I felt no pain. When I looked into the blistered, agony-wrenched faces that were screaming in pain, I heard nothing.

Every time I touched or moved a body, big patches of burned skin stuck to my hands; I had to constantly wipe my hands on my slacks. Once I pulled on a hand protruding from under a seat, but nothing was attached to it. I just dropped the hand and continued my search.

I felt nothing. I guess it was a self-defense shield to keep me from being overwhelmed by the ordeal. There was no way my conscious mind could handle the horror; so it refused delivery on most of the sensory messages coming in.

The one thing my mind didn't block out was the screeching of dozens of sirens, which seemed to wail on and on for eternity. Perhaps my mind used the screaming sirens to overload and short-circuit my senses and shut out everything else.

Within minutes I was aware of a host of emergency workers around me. They too sorted through the crumpled sheets of aluminum and dragged bodies away from the crash. "Help has arrived!" I realized, feeling my first tinge of relief.

Suddenly I felt the urgent need to go to the bathroom. So I headed toward another house. To get there I had to walk through a gathering cluster of spectators who stood on the road and gawked at the carnage.

"Don't just stand there," I screamed. "*Do* something! Pray! Do something!" Anger surged through me. But they only shifted their attention to me for a moment before turning to stare again at the rescue workers combing the crash.

A woman stood in her yard. I headed toward her. "I have to use your bathroom."

"Follow me, honey," she motioned, leading me into her home.

When I finished in the bathroom, the woman was waiting for me—with a cold wet washcloth and a hairbrush. She gently bathed my face, the washcloth turning black with soot by the time she finished. Then she brushed my hair back and fixed a pony-tail with a rubber band.

I thanked her and hurried back outside once again.

By this time even more ambulances had gathered at the top of the hill. Dozens of firefighters hosed down the larger pieces of the plane. Emergency workers carried stretchers at a trot toward the waiting ambulances. Others carried bodies toward a big yellow schoolbus that had been pulled onto a small gravel driveway among the trees near the top of the crash site. From overhead sounded the whomp-whomp-whomp of a rescue helicopter.

With no particular purpose in mind, I walked toward the line of emergency vehicles at the top of the hill. I couldn't escape the nagging feeling that there was something more I ought to be doing—some further responsibility I had to carry out. But I couldn't think.

"Am I alive?" I asked a nurse who was loading a passenger onto an ambulance.

Turning to look at me, she smiled. "Yes," she nodded. "You're all right."

I wasn't so sure. I made her touch me. The pressure of her hand on my arm felt warmly reassuring.

The nurse tried to talk me into one of the ambulances. A paramedic with her took my arm and tried to coax me to get on a stretcher. But I protested. "I'm okay. I'm okay. I'm one of the flight attendants, and I can identify pieces of the plane no one else would recognize. I can help you find bodies. I have to stay."

Insisting on my responsibility as a crew member, I finally thought of my undone duty. I realized what it was that I needed to do before I could leave the scene. "I have to find the rest of the crew." I didn't know I'd been thinking aloud until the nurse responded, "We'll go with you."

So she followed as two ambulance attendants picked me up and carried me through the woods, along a tiny stream and toward the far end of the crash site where I was sure I'd find the cockpit.

My rescue workers wanted to protect my lacerated feet, but I finally convinced them to let me down.

For several minutes I looked for something resembling the cabin door. But all I found were more bodies and gore. Rushing from one clump of smoldering wreckage to another, I happened on a large patch of charred earth. And there in the middle of the burned area was a body, charred stiff in a distorted U-shape. The arms, legs, head, and even the torso were off the ground, straining heavenward. And across the middle of the body lay the live power line that had created the scene.

Uncertain whether the corpse was male or female, I stared for a moment. Then, deciding it didn't matter, I backed away and resumed my own search for the crew.

Finally I spotted the nose of the plane. "Over there," I shouted and began to run. But the sight I found when I reached it stopped me cold.

The front of the plane had been ripped off in front of the cabin door. Lyman, the first officer, still sat strapped in his seat as it dangled from what was left of the cockpit. He was staring straight ahead with his eyes wide open, his face expressionless.

The captain lay on the ground just a little way away, his face mutilated almost beyond recognition. I fell to my knees beside him and cried, "Bill, Bill!" In what seemed like a natural reaction at that moment, I put my hands over his face and pressed the pieces back together in an attempt to lend a semblance of dignity to his death. He was my friend, and I couldn't leave him like that.

That's when I felt hands grabbing me. Four men pulled me away as I kicked and fought. "Cover him up!" I screamed. "At least have the decency to cover him up!"

Back on the road, the men set me down. But I took off again, running toward the yellow schoolbus, where a cluster of emergency personnel were working. There, among the trees, lay row after row of sheet-draped bodies. I walked between them to the rear of the bus, where men were loading stretchers through the emergency door. I looked in at the bodies already stacked inside. Then I turned and slowly surveyed the nightmare around me—the smoke, the broken metal, the shrouded dead, and the expression-less faces of the rescue workers who were also fighting to deny the horror of the scene.

Two more stretcher-bearers climbed the hill with a load. When they approached, I looked to see if I could recognize the body. But there wasn't any body—only *pieces* of bodies, collected from the wreckage.

That awful, gut-wrenching sight finally cracked my emotional shield. I felt strength drain out of me with a gush. And I put both hands to my head and began to shake.

"Get me out of here!" I wailed. "Get me out of here! I just can't look anymore."

Again I felt the firm hands. This time I surrendered to them. A man lifted me in his arms and trotted toward the road, clutching me to his chest. He handed me to another man who carried me a little farther and passed me to another, then another. Within moments I was transported back up the hill. The last man to take me wore the uniform of the Georgia State Patrol. He set me gently in the back seat of his patrol car before he climbed in, turned on his siren and flashers, and pulled quickly away from the crash site.

Racing down that little country road, we met what seemed like an endless procession of more police cars, ambulances and fire-trucks, sirens screaming, heading for the crash. They and the rolling Georgia terrain whizzed past in a blur.

"What's your name?" I asked, in an attempt to be friendly.

"Phil," the trooper responded.

"Hi, I'm Sandy."

The conversation got no further. We reached the first houses in the town of Dallas, Georgia. Moments later the patrol car pulled to a halt at the emergency doors of Paulding Memorial Hospital.

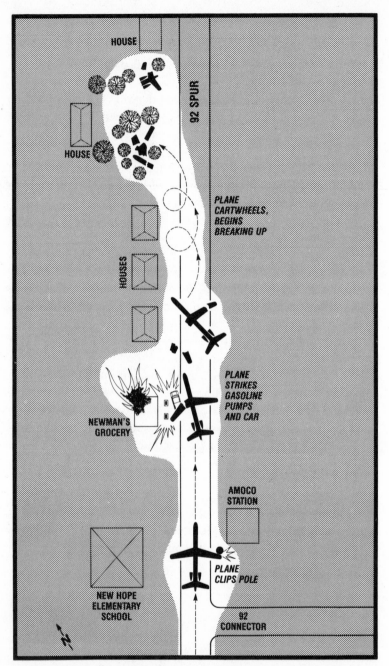

A diagram of the path of Flight 242 as the DC-9 careens down Highway Spur 92 through New Hope, Georgia. (actual site pictured opposite page.)

An aerial view of New Hope, Georgia, the morning after the crash. (*Photo by Bill Mahan*)

The wreckage of the tail section where Sandy was sitting.
(Photo by Billy Downs)

A view of the tail section and left engine, the first to lose power
prior to the crash. *(Photo by Billy Downs)*

A front view of Sandy's section. Her escape route through the flames led her straight through the middle debris. *(Photo by AP/World Wide Photos)*

The front galley of the plane. The cockpit was torn off just in front of the passenger door. Cathy, the other flight attendant, escaped from this section. *(Photo by Billy Downs)*

The mid-section of the aircraft. *(Photo by AP/World Wide Photos)*

A close-up of the left engine. An investigator notes the large dents in the cone made by hailstones. *(Photo by Billy Downs)*

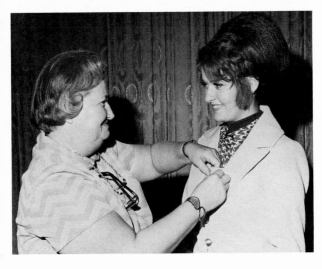

Dorothy Purl pins flight wings on Sandy, her daughter, at her 26 January 1973 graduation from flight attendant training.

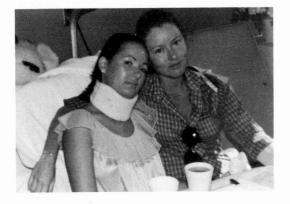

Lynnanne Sweeney, a Southern flight attendant comrade, visits Sandy in the Georgia Baptist Hospital in Atlanta in April 1977, just days after the crash.

Sandy's first flying lesson at Southexpressway Airport, Jonesboro, Georgia, in October 1978.

The graduating class from the first half of medical assistant school in Denver in May 1978. Sandy is standing in the middle.

On Sandy's first Southern flight, about eighteen months after the crash, a ground agent gives her a ride during a layover between Atlanta and Washington, D.C. *(Photo by Cecil Hare)*

Sandy models a 1963
vintage flight
attendant's uniform at a
Republic Airlines Open
House in Atlanta on
6 October 1984.

Sandy and her
husband, Robert C.
McAfee, on their
wedding day, March 14,
1983 in Atlanta.

A finalist in the first annual "Flight Attendant of the Year" competition held 19 September 1985 in New Orleans. Sandy receives a plaque from Henry L. Kotkins, Jr., President of Skyway Luggage.

Chapter 4

I slid out of the patrol car and walked into the hospital under my own power. Stepping through the emergency doors, I was greeted by a scene of controlled chaos.

Only a week before, this little hospital had conducted a disaster drill; Paulding Memorial Hospital couldn't have been more ready. A small army of doctors, nurses, and technicians bustled in and out of the four small examining rooms strung along the left side of a short hall. Everything seemed to be in constant motion as people dashed in, out, and around with clipboards, papers, instruments, and equipment.

For a minute I simply stood and watched the commotion.

But when I started across the hall toward the admissions desk, I heard a voice call, "Sandy!" I turned to see a stretcher pushed against the hallway wall. On that stretcher lay a grotesquely burned human form. I stepped close enough to see blistered lips barely moving and to hear a man's voice saying, "Help me. I taste blood and my finger hurts."

The combined feelings of compassion and helplessness churned inside me. This man had cried out to me because he remembered my name. I was a familiar face, representing hope. Yet I could do nothing to help him. And I doubted the doctors could.

I tried to smile. "You probably chipped a tooth. But you're in the hospital now, and you'll be all right."

"Thank you, Sandy," he whispered. "Thank you."

A nurse approached and rescued me from any more lies. "What's your name, miss?" she asked.

When I said, "Sandy Purl," I heard a shriek from one of the examining rooms. And a voice cried, "Sandy!"

I knew the voice was Cathy's, the other flight attendant. I rushed toward the room, yet just as I reached the open door of the examining room, I froze. I couldn't bring myself to see Cathy if she were badly burned.

27

But a split second later she burst into the hall, screaming, "Sandy, Sandy!" She threw her arms around me, and we both began to sob as we clung to each other in relief. Cathy was all right.

The nurse asked me to step into one of the examining rooms, but I refused to be treated until all the passengers had been cared for. I still felt responsibility. "I'm okay," I insisted.

Seeing the nurse wasn't going to argue, I asked where we could find a pay phone to call our families. After listening to her directions, I took Cathy by the arm and led her out of the emergency room, through two long, hospital-green hallways, and up a ramp to the lobby.

I dialed Mike in New Orleans. The instant I heard his voice, I blurted out, "I'm alive. I'm alive."

Mike had no idea what was going on. He hadn't heard the news. A full minute passed before I calmed down enough to explain that my plane had crashed and that I was okay.

But gradually I regained control. I told Mike which flight to catch out of New Orleans and told him to hurry or he'd miss the plane. I also asked him to bring me a pair of shoes—I'd lost mine in the crash.

After talking to Mike, I called my twin sister in Atlanta. When Candy answered, my emotions broke through again. Once more I could say nothing more important than "I'm alive, I'm alive!" as I cried into the receiver.

"Sandy! Oh, Sandy, thank God!" Candy sobbed into the phone on her end. "Where are you? Are you all right? Oh, Sandy! I heard about the crash on the way home! Where are you?"

But for a few minutes, again I just wept.

"Mama's here," said Candy, finally, after I had managed to blurt out where I was. "And she'll be coming to you as fast as she can get there, and David's coming with her. I've got to stay with Aprill."

Wiping my wet face on my sleeve, I managed, between sobs, to tell Candy how much I loved her, and how afraid I'd been that I would never see anyone I loved again.

Once I'd informed my family of my safety, I tried to contact Southern Airways' offices in Atlanta. The lines were busy, so I tried again and again. In flight attendant training, I'd been drilled that I must inform Southern immediately in the event of any accident. Like caring for passengers, it was part of my job.

After countless unsuccessful attempts to get through, I even called the reservation office of Delta to ask them to relay a message. But no one could help. I finally gave up, but not without feeling some guilt.

For the next hour I walked with Cathy from one end of the hospital to the other. Nurses kept asking me to sit down, but I couldn't stay still. So I walked and talked—nonstop—to elderly patients we saw in the halls, to nurses who kept checking up on us, and to Cathy. I don't remember much of what was said, but I do recall asking Cathy if she'd seen the cockpit crew.

"They're dead," she replied.

"I know," I told her, and we let the subject drop.

Finally a nurse found us to say all the passengers had been treated and the doctors were ready for me in the emergency room. We followed her back through the hospital, down the long basement corridor, and out again into the emergency wing.

I sat on the edge of an examination table as one of the staff doctors checked me out from head to toe. My only evident injuries were the cuts on my feet, second-degree burns on the front of my legs where I'd bumped against hot metal pieces of the aircraft, and a few minor burns around my neck and temples where my hair had been singed.

No sooner had my examination concluded than one of the vice-presidents of Southern, Sam Brady, stepped into the room. "Hi, Sandy," he said. "Are you okay?"

I was so relieved to see someone from Southern I jumped off the table, threw myself into his arms, and began to cry. He held me and patted my back, saying, "You're okay, Sandy. Everything is going to be fine, now."

Mr. Brady and another Southern Airways official led Sandy and Cathy to a nearby room and began asking questions about the crash. But before the women could get completely through their accounts, the two men were called away. Cathy and Sandy waited for a while. But

when the men didn't return, a nurse eventually came to escort them to
regular hospital rooms where they would spend the night.

The staff assigned them rooms on the maternity ward because secu-
rity was tighter there. They wanted to protect the two crew members
from the dozens of reporters who were already besieging the hospital
and asking to talk to survivors of the crash.

When I got to my room, two aides helped me to the shower to
get cleaned up. For a long time I just let the clean warm water
soothe me before I began trying to remove the dirt and the smell
of smoke from my body. I was almost done when I dropped the
bar of soap. When I reached down to pick it up I saw pieces of my
hair on the floor of the shower. My mind flashed back to the smell
of burning hair and the fireball that had streaked through the cabin on first impact.

I screamed and felt myself go limp. But the aides grabbed me
and helped me out of the shower and into a hospital gown. After
that incident, I refused to be left alone in my room. So, at my insis-
tence, the nurses moved a cot into Cathy's room for me. Even then
I couldn't keep still. I paced the room and relived the crash in my
mind.

When nurses came in, I grilled them about the survivors. They
tried to reassure me all the passengers had been cared for and sent
on to other hospitals in Atlanta. When one of them admitted that
one man remained at Paulding, I badgered her until I found out
where he was. The moment I heard his room number, I was off to
see him for myself. I didn't care that my backside showed out the
back of my hospital gown as I ran down the hall. I just had to see
my passenger.

The man was sitting on his bed eating his supper when I went
dashing into his room. His hands were bandaged, but I could tell
he was going to be all right. I was so happy to see one of the passengers in such good shape that I jumped up on the bed beside the
man, threw my arms around him, and cried with relief.

By the time the nurses caught up with me, I'd regained some
control of my emotions. They led me back down the halls to
Cathy's room.

My feelings escaped me again late in the evening when my mother arrived. The moment I saw the short broad figure pause at the door of Cathy's room, I ran to her, hugged her and cried uncontrollably for a few minutes as she held me. When I stopped crying, I started talking for the first time about the details of the crash. My mother just listened and held me. From time to time I'd sit up and pull away to look into that loving face with the rosy cheeks and the familiar blue eyes. Then I'd surrender to the comfort of her arms.

The nurses came back and tried to convince me to go to my own room. But I told them I didn't want to leave Cathy alone, so we stayed. I asked my mother to help me get the smoke and burned smell out of my hair. When we finished in the bathroom, I kept right on talking until well past midnight.

Through it all, my mother maintained the composure and strength of an experienced army nurse.

When the hospital staff learned my mother had been a military nurse, they entrusted her with a heavy dose of Valium to see if she could get me to sleep. I was still fighting the drugs when Mike finally arrived at three o'clock in the morning. When he walked into the room, I leaped to my feet and promptly collapsed in his arms. For the first time since the crash, I quit trying to hold the feelings in check. I let them all go and cried until I exhausted my entire body. Mike finally carried me into my own room and put me in bed. My mother wanted to come with me too, but I asked her to stay with Cathy until someone came for her.

I remember very little of the remaining hours of my stay at Paulding; I guess the drugs numbed my mind. But I didn't sleep. Each time I'd doze off, I'd see fire and bodies and wake up screaming. Sometime before dawn the shock began to wear off, and I began to feel excruciating pain. Every muscle in my body, especially in my back and neck, seemed to have been torn loose.

When I cried out with pain, a nurse hurried in to give me a shot. But the morphine only lessened my desire to scream. The pain didn't seem to retreat one bit.

When the doctors came around the next morning, they told Sandy she'd be checking out of Paulding and going to a hospital in Atlanta. The actual transfer was like something out of an old spy movie. Soon after her twin sister Candy arrived, the hospital announced to the press that Sandy would be moving. They even brought an ambulance around to the front entrance where all the TV cameras and reporters were waiting. Then Sandy was whisked out the back door and loaded into another ambulance. Candy, Mike, and a representative from Southern Airways climbed in with her, and the vehicle took off. Driving through the crowded parking lot, everyone in the ambulance laughed about the horde of reporters watching the front door for Sandy's departure.

By early afternoon Sandy was an official patient at Georgia Baptist Hospital in Atlanta. Most of her stay there is only a faint blur in her memory, though she does vividly recall a couple incidents and eventually reconstructed a few others with the help of family and friends who were with her.

I guess I amazed the doctors and nurses. Despite heavy doses of thorazine and morphine, I wouldn't sleep. I think I was afraid to let go of consciousness because I was afraid to loosen the tight grip I had to keep on my emotions every waking second. And I knew I couldn't control the dreams.

After three long days, I did fall deeply asleep. This time, when the dreams came, I awakened in terror to find my room crowded with doctors and nurses.

I screamed, "What's the matter?" At least, I *thought* I screamed: one of the nurses bent close to my face and asked if I'd said something. I heard myself whisper, "What's the matter?" I thought I was dead.

"You're okay, Sandy," the nurse smiled. "It's just the first time you've slept in three days, and you look so peaceful."

I didn't believe her. I insisted everyone in the room touch me before I could be convinced I wasn't dead.

Although the hospital turned away most of the people who came to see me, I still had a constant stream of visitors. To most of them, I appeared fine. I calmly told the story of the crash—at least, some of the story—again and again, in response to dozens of curious questions.

But I was a desperate actress playing a part. I tried to lock my real fears and feelings into my inner world—a world that began to torment and terrify me. Sometimes I'd let my defenses sag, or something unexpected would break through them; when that happened, the people who were with me would catch a glimpse into the hell raging inside me.

My room at the Georgia Baptist was located directly above the emergency entrance. The sounds of incoming ambulances never failed to trigger a flashback. Sometimes four people were needed to hold me down as I kicked and screamed through the torture of a wailing siren.

The constant vigilance required to try to suppress memories and emotions took so much effort that I couldn't always separate the hospital reality from those memories. A bell would go off in the night and I'd run up and down the hall, trying to evacuate patients by pulling them out of bed. Nurses would walk into my room in the dark, and I'd scream, "Grab your ankles!" and keep screaming until they obeyed.

One night a friend walked into the room as I lay in semidarkness. Absentmindedly he picked up the television remote control and changed the station. For an instant the room flickered red in the glow of the picture, and all I could think was "Fire!"

I screamed and kept screaming until my twin, Candy, threw her arms around me and told me again and again, "It's only the TV, Sandy. It's only the TV."

One day, after I'd been in the hospital for several days, an executive from Southern's headquarters dropped in to see me.

"I have some of your things, Sandy," she said in greeting.

Then without another word, she marched to my bed, where I was propped up, and lifted a small Southern Airways trashbag over my lap and ceremoniously upturned the contents.

A charred wallet book and a mud-caked New Testament that had belonged to my father were the only recognizable pieces. Soot and little clods of dried red clay scattered across the white sheet. I sat in stunned silence for a moment, looking at the woman's expressionless face.

"I don't believe it. I don't believe you did that." My voice level rose with each repetition of the phrase. Two nurses hurried from the hall where they had been talking with Mike. He took one look at the mess on my lap and stood to challenge the woman face to face. "Get out," he ordered and roughly shoved her toward the door. As she disappeared into the hall I swore and yelled, "I'll have your job for this!"

Mike and the nurses quickly cleared the remains from my bed. But I shook with rage for half an hour after she was gone. What had she thought she was doing? A kindness? Or was she eager to feed off the smell of disaster that clung to me?

None of my emotions were under control. So even those closest to me suffered from attacks of my rage. Because smoke triggered flashbacks, for example, I lashed out at anyone who stepped into the room with a cigarette.

Sometimes there was no real reason for my outbursts. I just vented my fears and frustration by striking out at the nearest targets.

One day my mother walked around the room reading some of the cards from well-wishers that had come to me, along with seventy bouquets and a menagerie of stuffed animals. When she got to the window ledge, my mother (who was a heavy woman) sorted through a pile of candy boxes there. Pulling out a box of Russell Stover divinity, she said, "Oh Sandy—here's one box I'd like to keep."

For no reason I exploded: "What the hell do you want with that? You're nothing but big and fat and gloppy anyway!"

She said nothing in response, but I could see in her face that my barb had gone deep. Silently she walked out of the room. A long time passed before she returned, and neither of us ever acknowledged the incident again.

I was oblivious to the pain I inflicted on the people around me. I never once considered the demands I placed on my mother or Mike, who were with me almost all day, every day. Nor did I stop to appreciate my sisters, who would rush to the hospital whenever I called and insisted, "I have to see you right away."

An exception came when Mike's four-year-old son Ryan called

for the first time after the crash. He asked, "How are you?" And I told him I was fine. Then he wanted to know, "Sandy, do you still have all your arms and legs?" And I remember a warm feeling of gratitude for his childish concern, which prompted me to try to reassure him that I was indeed going to be all right, that I still had all my arms and legs. When he hung up, I began to cry for all those who didn't.

I talked with my family and with the many visitors who came. I talked a lot with two of my fellow flight attendants, Donna Alleman and Karan Wesson, who gave up several days of their own time to sit with me in my room and give my family a break. I watched television. I even compiled my own scrapbook of all the newspaper accounts of the crash. But I did it all without really thinking. The only reality, the one thing that consumed me was the continuing battle against the memories and emotions inside me that seemed too horrible and too powerful to let out or to face.

But I was losing that battle. And I was scared.

Chapter 5

The person I wanted and needed most to be sitting beside me in that hospital room was my father. I needed his strength, his steadiness, in my out-of-control world. The most vivid and recent image I had of him was from the crash, as he stood with me looking down at my trapped, unconscious body.

While that experience had given me an overwhelming peace at the time, my *memory* of the encounter was anything but peaceful. For one thing, trying to relive the memory brought back all the related emotions of the trauma. And because I could imagine no reasonable explanation for the encounter with my father, I saw it as possible evidence that I was mentally cracking up. I didn't dare mention the incident to anyone for fear they'd confirm the insanity I was beginning to suspect.

Despite regular injections of morphine and thorazine, the pain in my neck and back never left. Yet the doctors seemed to think I was getting physically better. In physical therapy, I learned to maneuver on crutches to keep my weight off my healing feet. Almost two weeks after I arrived at Georgia Baptist, I was allowed to leave the hospital for a few hours to go out to dinner at my sister Sue's home.

We were on the way, Mike driving, when the muscles in my arms began to twitch. I didn't think much about it at first. Then the muscles in my legs started. As the spasms intensified, the pain took hold. By the time we reached Sue's, my whole body had gone into spasm and I was soaked with sweat. All I could do was cry and moan. Mike called the hospital and was instructed to bring me right back. All night long, while the nurses kept me in a hot bath to relieve the agony, I wondered what was going on. Not until the doctor arrived the next morning did I receive any explanation.

"We're easing you off morphine and thorazine," he said. "What you experienced was a typical case of drug withdrawal." He prescribed another drug he said would help relieve the physical reactions. But I decided not to take it, choosing instead to brave out the spasms with hot baths and massages.

Less than a week later, my doctors determined I was well enough to return to New Orleans. After one night there, in Tulane University Hospital, I was released to go home as an outpatient.

But even alone again with Mike, the emotions inside me still raced up and down like a runaway roller coaster.

The first three days at home brought a steady stream of phone calls and visits from both friends and reporters who wanted to talk with me about the crash. Those ceaseless intrusions only stirred and intensified the storm of related emotions raging inside me. Since I still couldn't talk rationally about any of it with Mike, we both decided I ought to get away. So a friend drove me to Ft. Walton, where I stayed in the apartment of another friend who was gone on vacation.

I spent most of my week-and-a-half stay in Florida alone at the beach, hoping to find peace in solitude. I remember awakening one afternoon to feel the warmth of the sand under my beach towel, the heat of the sun's rays penetrating clear to my bones. The thought struck me, "It's not so bad being dead."

Death seemed the most rational explanation for the feeling of aloneness I experienced in the confused, hybrid world of my own thoughts and reality. My fears and flashbacks were horribly real. Yet my friends and family never seemed to know or respond to what was so clearly happening in my mind. It made no sense unless I was a ghost who could see but not be seen.

When Sandy returned to New Orleans, she still couldn't talk about the crash for fear of unleashing uncontrollable emotions. And no one was telling Mike what to expect or how to respond. He couldn't cope any better with his wife's fluctuating emotions than she could. As his frustration and sense of hopelessness grew, he began to complain about something he'd shielded Sandy from since the crash—Southern's response to their situation.

"Honey," he said, "look at this," He held out a sheaf of yellow, lined legal paper.

"I just don't know where these folks get off," he said. "See, here—when you were at Georgia Baptist, I called to get them to pay my hotel, and all they said was that I should stay with your sister Sue instead. I told them, that way I'd have to travel forty miles a day just to see you."

I looked at the writing on the page, feeling bewildered.

"But they *did* pay, didn't they?" I asked him.

"Yeah, eventually—the rental car, too. But that's not all." Mike flipped the page over and pointed at some notes he'd jotted down there.

"When your union rep came by," he said angrily, "this guy from Southern came in afterward and said you shouldn't be talking to the union. And one day, the same guy—I found him in there tape recording you. You were all drugged up, and yelling."

My eyes ached, and I felt sick.

"Well, but why didn't you tell me all this sooner?" I demanded.

"Honey," he retorted, "you were in no shape to hear *anything*!"

I knew that was probably true.

I knew I'd been so doped up in the hospital I couldn't remember much. But I couldn't believe what Mike was saying about the company and the people I worked for. There was already so much I couldn't understand or cope with; it was impossible to deal with Mike's charges. I'd had a longer relationship with Southern than I'd had with my husband. And since I couldn't imagine what he was up to, or why he'd want to ruin my reputation at the airline, I decided I could no longer trust him.

By the last week of May I decided I needed to get away from Mike again for a while. I knew the National Transportation Safety Board hearings were scheduled the first week of June, and I'd be required to testify. So I went to Atlanta to be with my family and prepare myself. For the first time in almost two months I was looking ahead; but I was terrified that I'd come completely apart on the witness stand.

I was with my twin, Candy, reviewing the scrapbook of newspaper clippings about the crash, when I came to an item naming five young children and three mothers who'd died in a car in front of Newman's Store. I exploded, "Who put this in here? Why didn't anyone tell me about the babies?"

Candy reacted with obvious surprise. "*You* cut the clipping out and put it in the book, Sandy. You put together all those clippings!"

I couldn't believe her. "Why didn't anyone tell me about the babies dying?" I asked.

"We *did* talk about it. You talked about it in the hospital." Candy insisted. "Don't you remember?"

I didn't remember. I didn't recall any of the clippings. So I quit arguing and continued reading. Except for the parts of the crash I'd experienced firsthand, the scrapbook read like a brand new story to me. As I poured over it in preparation for my testimony, the horrible impact of the crash on other people dawned on me for the first time.

For eight weeks I'd lived with my own personal tragedy—as if I'd been the sole survivor, the only victim. The truth slowly sank in—seventy-two dead, including nine citizens of the small community.

Sitting there, safe on the couch in Candy's living room, I thought about my passengers, about how they had trusted me and I hadn't been able to save them. I thought about the people of New Hope, who had done nothing to deserve the disaster we had dropped on their town. I even felt guilty for surviving when so many of those who died had families and children who had depended on them and all I had was Mike. And when I realized how little I had suffered in comparison to those who had died or to those survivors whose chances for a normal life were destroyed by burns and injuries, I felt more guilt over my inability to cope with my seemingly insignificant problems.

I began to see the upcoming hearings as my best hope for a new life. Despite the continuing fear that I might break down or become hysterical on the stand, I began to look forward to the hearing as the place where I would finally get everything out in the open. I would tell everything, just the way it had happened, including some details I knew Southern wouldn't want me to say.

That would absolve me of all my guilt. Maybe then the pain would go away.

The day before the hearings, Southern Airways called Sandy into company headquarters. One of the executives met with her and then took her to meet with three Southern attorneys he said wanted to review her testimony. The lawyers went over the six-and-a-half page preliminary statement Sandy had made to NTSB interviewers a couple of weeks earlier in New Orleans. And they asked some specific questions about her experience. They didn't come right out and say it in so many words, but Sandy felt as if they were trying to tell her what she was supposed to say on the stand. They said her testimony probably wouldn't last very long because Cathy was going to testify first, and they expected only a few routine follow-up questions for Sandy to fill in on.

It seemed obvious to me the lawyers wanted me to steer clear of any subject that might reflect poorly on Southern. I began to get a little angry.

When I asked if Cathy was in town yet, they told me she was. So I asked if I could see her. They said, "No. We wouldn't want you to get your stories confused." I tried to explain that I just wanted to see her, not talk about the crash. But they refused. And that made me angrier yet.

When we finished talking, the lawyers took me to the hotel where the hearing was scheduled. "We want you to see the room before tomorrow so you know what to expect," they said.

I expected some little seminar room. So when I walked into a ballroom filled with hundreds of chairs, my surprise stopped me in my tracks. The lawyers quickly indicated various tables where panel members would be sitting. When they pointed out the area reserved for the Transportation Workers Union representatives, I commented, "Then I'll be sitting there."

"Oh, no," one of the lawyers responded. "You won't be in the room when Cathy is testifying."

"What do you mean?" I asked.

"Well, um, you'll probably be in another room going over last-minute questions with us."

That's where I got good and mad. "I am going to be in this room when Cathy testifies. And I will be sitting right there, with my union." The attorneys didn't argue with me, but I saw them exchanging awkward looks. Our appointment was brought quickly to a close.

The next morning I walked into a hearing room crowded with cameras, reporters, and relatives of Flight 242 passengers. Also present, of course, were officials and lawyers for every company and organization connected with the crash: the aircraft manufacturer; the makers of the jet engines and the cockpit radar; the weather bureau; the controllers; the pilots and flight attendants' unions; Southern; and more I didn't even know about. I took my place with my union's representatives and waited for the proceedings to start.

Almost immediately Cathy was called to testify. But her answers were brief and sometimes indirect. I vowed to be as specific and as detailed as I could be. While her testimony continued about the events of April 4, I passed a note to one of the lawyers from Ralph Nader's organization, who was taking part in the inquiry. The note read, "Please be sure to direct all the questions asked of [Cathy] to me as well." And I'd signed it.

When the chairman of the hearing finally dismissed Cathy and I heard my own name called, I took a deep breath and walked determinedly to the stand. After a number of preliminary questions to establish my identity and work experience, the first questioner finally asked me to describe the day of the crash. I described the earlier flights briefly and then began talking about Flight 242 out of Huntsville. He stopped me every few seconds to ask about a detail here or a meaning there. And when I told about the engines going "Pow, Pow, Pow," he stopped me again and asked if there had been any strange engine noise prior to that. I said there hadn't been and began describing the sound of hail.

And for the next fifteen minutes straight I gave the most complete factual account I could of everything that happened. I told about the initial hailstorm: "All of a sudden, the entire plane was engulfed with pounding. The hail was so loud, when the left engine quit, I thought it had actually been ripped off the aircraft."

I told about briefing the passengers: "I knew we had no power. I smelled fire. I pictured the plane exploding . . . I had no idea of the intensity of the problem . . . I had not talked to Cathy. I had not been notified by the cockpit . . . I just got up and started briefing the passengers."

I gave a detailed account of my instructions about crash positions, window exits, and evacuation routes. and in describing my briefing to the passengers at the rear of the cabin, I said, "I thought I would be incapacitated totally. . . . I smelled fire . . . so I figured the back would explode on impact. So I told them just to push me out of the way, and explained how . . . to get the tail cone jettisoned and get people evacuating out the tail."

From time to time I hesitated, expecting my questioner to ask some point of clarification. But my first few pauses were met only by the silence that had settled over the room. So I'd start right in again. I described talking on the intercom with Cathy. And I recounted my experience through the moments of impact. I skipped the part about seeing my own body and encountering my father, but I did describe in detail my exit from the plane: "I started to walk forward and it was kind of like drawing the curtains on a stage. That's the best way I can describe it. The flames split down the middle, and I couldn't believe it. I walked through the flames and stepped into nothing. There was, there was no airplane there. . . . [it] had just been torn to shreds like a piece of tissue paper . . . There were bodies all over the place, but I proceeded to pull the passengers that were lying around to the side of the road away from the fire. . . . "

As my account continued to unfold, tears began to run down the faces of several panel members. A couple of times when I paused to attempt to keep my emotions in check, I could hear people sobbing at the tables and around the room. But I kept my story going right up to my arrival at Paulding Memorial Hospital and my encounter with the burned passenger waiting for emergency treatment. Finally I described my reunion with Cathy in the emergency ward and said, "We were together most of that evening until they separated us. I don't remember much after that."

Sandy stopped talking at that point. There was a long moment of continued silence before a chorus of audible sighs moved through the crowd like an exhaled breath.

The chairman of the hearing gave Sandy a couple of minutes to take a drink of water. Then the first questioner followed up with a few more specific questions about when exactly the auxiliary power unit kicked on, when the plane depressurized, and so on. Then the chair called for a ten-minute recess before the other questioners got a chance at Sandy.

As I stepped down from the stand, my eyes met those of one of the Southern Airways insurance representatives across the room. Even though I was instantly surrounded by family, friends, and other well-wishers, I kept eye contact with the official as he walked toward the crowd clustering around me. As he pushed his way right on past me without stopping, he said, "Stick to the questions. Don't elaborate."

I didn't have any damning evidence against Southern. But I had determined to tell everything there was to tell. So when I resumed the stand and other questioners asked me about our schedule for the day of April 4, I told the truth. I said we hadn't had a legal break the night before. Officially we were short of the required eight-hour layover by just a few minutes, but what with the bad weather and the trips to and from the motel in Muscle Shoals, we'd only had about six hours sleep. I told about Captain McKenzie saying he was going to call Southern the night of April 3 and ask permission to stay in Huntsville instead of flying on to Muscle Shoals in bad weather and risking an illegal layover.

Before I knew it, the questioners were done and the chairman of the hearings was thanking me for testifying under such trying circumstances. I was dismissed, and the hearing was adjourned for lunch.

Again as I stepped down from the stand a crowd gathered around me. A short, slightly balding, middle-aged man walked up to me and quietly asked if he could speak to me. He pulled out a wallet photo of himself and a woman—obviously his wife.

"Do you remember where she was sitting on the plane?" he asked.

I realized he just wanted some word of recognition or assurance from one of the last people to have seen his wife alive. So I racked my brain to remember her. Finally I shook my head. "I know there were only a few women on the plane. But I just can't remember."

He nodded and started to turn away. But I reached out and hugged him. And I kissed him lightly on the cheek. That was all the comfort I could offer him.

Just after that a woman approached me. "I lost my mother in the crash," she told me. "And for a long time I had trouble dealing with her death. I couldn't accept the way she'd died, with her body mangled, burned, and torn. But then someone gave me this," and she held out a book. "After I read it, I sensed some of the peace my mother must have gained in death.

"I know some of the feelings you must be going through. And I'd like you to have this book." She opened the cover to show me where she'd written her mother's name before she pressed the book into my hands.

Here was a woman who had lost a mother, and *she* was trying to comfort *me*—a survivor. I was deeply moved by her compassion. I thanked her with tears running down my face.

I took the book and placed it with my papers and things without really looking at it again to see what it was about.

The only thing I could think about as I walked out of that ball-room was the relief I felt that I'd survived the hearings. Again and again I joyfully declared to myself, "I did it. I did it." I'd told my story of the crash for the first time—at least I'd told the facts, if not my feelings—and I'd done it all without falling apart.

Maybe now I could go on with my life.

Chapter 6

I spent the night in the Georgian Terrace Hotel, only a few floors above the hearings room—with plans to stay for the subsequent days of testimony. The next morning, June 7, 1977, I awakened late, dressed in a rush before grabbing a quick cup of coffee from the hotel coffee shop, and reached the crowded ballroom just before the hearings began their second day.

Many friends and even more strangers greeted me as I wound my way through the crowd. And when I finally found a seat near the union table, one of the TWU representatives said, "Congratulations on your great job yesterday, Sandy. You even made the morning paper."

"What do you mean?"

She handed me a copy of the *Atlanta Constitution*. I unfolded it to see a front-page, full-color picture of myself on the witness stand. Bigger even than the name of the paper was the headline: "Flames Just Parted." The subhead read, "Stewardess Recalls the Moments Before and After Flight 242 Crashed in New Hope." And under my photo was my name and a quote about my briefing of the passengers. "I Told Them Not to Worry About Me."

The front-page story led by retelling my post-testimony encounter with the man who showed me the wallet photo of his wife. I'd had no idea anyone had witnessed that conversation, and here it was plastered on the front page of the newspaper for all the world to read. I wept again for the man's pain as I read the reporter's account.

According to the newspaper, my story, "told to a crowd of more than 200 aviation professionals and newsmen in a stiflingly-hot hearing room, was the most dramatic moment of the first day's hearing into the causes of the crash." The article went on to quote long portions of my testimony.

It was like reading someone else's words; I didn't remember

anything about the testimony except my determination to tell everything, and the tidal wave of relief that had flooded over me when I had finished. Reading it all in that newspaper, sitting in that hearing room, resurrected such vivid images in my mind, that I shook too much to hold the paper still enough to read the other articles on the hearings.

Sandy's testimony made front-page headlines that day in newspapers across the Southeast. Article after article reported her calm professionalism before the crash and her determination to help her passengers in the aftermath. Additional testimony throughout the hearings, from surviving passengers and rescue workers, credited her for her courage and her devotion to duty. One man testifying at the hearing told about her moving pieces of the plane and pulling bodies out of the wreckage. "She made the bionic woman look like Shirley Temple," he said. By the time the hearings concluded and Sandy went back to New Orleans a few days later, millions of people had read her story and considered her a heroine.

I didn't feel like a heroine. Some of the initial relief I'd felt after my testimony still remained. But instead of putting the crash behind me once and for all, my public recounting of it and the days of preparation for my testimony had brought everything to the surface, including the most personal emotions and experiences during the crash that I had yet to tell anyone. After the hearing, the vision (or whatever it had been) of my father, and vivid sensory images I'd only recalled in horrible nightmares, began to regularly plague my conscious mind.

The evidence at the hearings did relieve some of my guilt feelings, at least on an intellectual level. Eighteen of the twenty-one survivors had been passengers in my section, following my instructions. And after hearing other accounts of my actions at the crash site, I didn't know what more I could have done there.

I went back to New Orleans and to Mike after the hearings. I needed and wanted my husband's comfort. Yet, because I'd never asked Mike to be a comforter before, I didn't know how to express my need. I'd always prided myself in being strong; I feared his rejection if he saw how confused and weak I really was.

And after so many weeks of desperately trying to keep the flood of uncontrollable feelings dammed up inside, I found it impossible to release even a little warmth and love for Mike for fear a torrent of emotion would burst through and wipe out my sanity, my marriage, everything. So I couldn't, or wouldn't, respond to him emotionally or physically.

I knew Mike couldn't answer all the "Why?" questions any better than I could. So I didn't even share that most basic inner struggle with him. Taking his cue from my avoidance of the subject, I guess the only way he knew to try to help me was to try to act as if the crash never happened. But of course pretending didn't work.

My own problems consumed so much of my emotional energy, there was nothing left for our crumbling marriage. So after only a few days in New Orleans, I loaded all my personal belongings in a U-Haul and moved back to Atlanta. Mike reluctantly let me go and hired a man to drive my things back to Atlanta.

Going back to Atlanta felt like the best thing that had happened to me since April 4. I moved in temporarily with a long-time girlfriend, Carla. She and I had gone to high school together and had even worked our first jobs together, at our local Dairy Queen. She'd seen me through the loss of my father and a lot of other hard times. She knew me, and as a Southern Airways employee working in the accounting department, she also knew a lot about the accident. So she knew a lot without me having to say much about what I was going through. That made her place an ideal refuge for me, an ideal base from which to rebuild some order in my life.

Soon after my return to Atlanta, I engaged a law firm to represent me in any settlement resulting from the crash. Mike had already enlisted an attorney, but since we were temporarily separated, I felt I needed someone to exclusively look out for my interests. I signed on the Washington, D.C., firm of Smiley and Lear, lawyers I'd met at the NTSB hearing.

In a new effort to deal with the unrelenting fears and emotions still plaguing me, I began visiting a therapist. As a result, I felt I was slowly but surely regaining some control of my life.

Then I got a letter at Carla's. Registered mail. I signed for it and retreated into the living room. Quickly tearing open the envelope with the familiar Southern Airways logo, I unfolded and scanned the tersely worded paragraphs as I sank down into one padded easy chair. There had to be some mistake. As a knot tightened in my stomach, I began to read again from the beginning, hoping I had misunderstood the message.

The letter informed me that Cathy, the other flight attendant on Southern Flight 242, was going back on the line as a flight attendant as of the first of the month. And while the company had continued to pay both of our regular salaries since the crash, my regular pay would be discontinued as of July 1 and I would receive only worker's compensation until such time as I could resume full-time duties.

I'd read the letter right the first time. Southern was cutting off my pay. In shocked disbelief, I called Carla, my sister Candy, my lawyer, and my union rep. The surprise and dismay expressed by each of them bolstered my hopes. "It must be a mistake," I said each time I hung up.

The next afternoon I parked my car outside Southern Airways headquarters and walked into the building for an appointment with Sam Brady, the Southern vice-president who'd embraced me in the emergency room of Paulding Memorial Hospital the night of April 4. When he'd come to visit me later at Georgia Baptist Hospital, I'd expressed concern about being able to make my car payments and he'd reassured me: "Now, don't you worry, Sandy. Your car payments will be taken care of if I have to pay for them out of my own pocket."

So as the secretary ushered me into the vice-president's office I had no doubts Brady would stand by me until we got the whole thing ironed out. He greeted me warmly and called for an executive I'd never met to join us. Once we were all settled, Brady picked up a letter from his desk and handed it to me. "Who's this man?" he asked.

I took a quick look at the letterhead and replied, "He's the lawyer I've gotten to represent me in any legal developments resulting from the crash."

"Should he be here today?" Brady asked.

"No, sir," I replied. "I told my lawyer and the union I wanted to come by myself to get some explanation about the letter I received saying my pay is being cut off."

At that point, Brady leaned back in his chair and looked me in the eye for a few seconds. "I just have one bit of advice for you, Sandy," he said. "You shouldn't bite the hand that feeds you."

I don't know that another plane crash could have devastated me any more than those words. I only vaguely remember the rest of the meeting during which Brady and the other official explained how the company had generously paid my salary since the crash, even though they hadn't been required by the flight attendant union's contract to do so. They assured me they certainly hoped I would be able to return to work very soon. But in the meantime they were sure I'd understand that they couldn't continue to pay me if I couldn't work.

I walked out of that office feeling brutally betrayed and very much alone. Was I being punished for telling the truth at the hearings? What other explanation was there?

Sandy immediately called her lawyer and the TWU to report on her meeting. The union was deep in negotiations with management over a new contract; someone looking for publicity leaked the news of her pay cutoff to the press. So a couple of days later Sandy once again found herself the subject of front-page news. The report told of Southern's plan to cut off her pay. In the story, a Southern Airways spokesman referred to Sandy as "a disgruntled employee."

When friends and colleagues from Southern called Sandy to check the validity of the story, she told them about the letter. But the company posted a carefully worded official Telex on the employee bulletin board citing incomplete or erroneous information from the union and the press, and stating (truthfully at that point) that Ms. Purl "has received full pay and benefits and continues to do so. Although we asked her, by letter, to meet with us to discuss either a return to work or acceptance of workman's compensation . . . " The notice implied that Sandy and/or the union officials were using misinformation to further their own ends.

Feeling betrayed by my company was bad enough. But being publicly discredited was far worse. I spent the rest of the summer in alternate states of confusion, guilt, and anger.

The confusion set in every time, thousands of times, I asked myself "Why?" Why the crash? Why did I survive? Why did my marriage have to disintegrate? Why did the company want to cut me off? Why did I have to get caught between management and the union in contract negotiations?

I thought a lot about the crash in New Hope. I remembered walking back and forth along the road, clenching and unclenching my fists, telling myself to stay calm so I could do my duty. I'd wanted to do everything I could.

I repeatedly berated myself: "What didn't I do? The company must know something I did wrong. Why else would they treat me like this? That has to be it. The company trusted me and my passengers trusted me. And all those people died. I couldn't help them, and they died." Again and again I grieved for those deaths and for my own sense of guilt. When I wasn't struggling with bouts of confusion and guilt, I was consumed by anger.

One day I was with some flight attendant friends when one of them said something about a Southern executive. I exploded with as long a string of curse words as I could muster. I damned Southern and everyone in management to hell and kept up my foulmouthed attack until I noticed my friends exchanging uncomfortable glances and staring at the floor.

My anger was never far from the surface. Under pressure from the union and public opinion, the company did continue my pay. But as the summer wore on, the mere sound of the name "Southern" would trigger a bitter tirade. It wasn't long before I was telling Carla if I had my way I'd blow up Southern headquarters and everyone in it. And I meant it. In the deepest depths of my heart, I meant it.

Not too surprisingly, most of Sandy's old friends began avoiding her. Not even her most faithful friends and her family were ever sure how to act. They wanted to comfort and support her, but they were always afraid they would say something or do something that would send her plunging into despair or erupting into rage. Sandy had become a stranger, and she felt their uncertainty and awkwardness. Their withdrawal intensified her feelings of aloneness.

For all these reasons, Sandy became more and more dependent on her therapist. At least once a week, and sometimes as often as three times, she went in for an appointment with the psychologist. He helped her talk about and channel her anger. He became an advocate for Sandy with Southern, writing letters on her behalf and trying to explain to the company executives her need for their support. Without trying to defend them, he tried to help Sandy understand a little about the corporate perspective. Southern had never had an incident like this before; the company had no idea of the needs of a surviving flight attendant. Southern did offer Sandy a full-time spot in air freight, but her physician had said her neck and back weren't ready for any job that required working over a desk all day. Through all this discussion, Sandy's counselor played the supportive role of mediator and go-between whenever he could.

My therapist was the one person I could unload on. The one person who would listen to me vent my anger without squirming, who would listen without alarm to my talk about bombing Southern. The one person who had accepted me the way I was, without longing for the old Sandy, who had died in the plane crash.

We didn't ever get down to my feelings and memories about the crash itself; we were too busy dealing with my immediate anger and reaction to the airline. But we did talk some about my family and my father's death, and I was beginning to think if there was any hope for understanding and living with the trauma of the crash, therapy would provide the answer.

It wasn't as though my friends and family didn't try to encourage me. From time to time during the summer, one or the other of my sisters would embrace me and cry for no apparent reason, as if they were overcome with sympathy for my pain or gratitude for my survival. But their emotion, meant as a comfort, only reminded me that my reactions were disrupting the lives of the people I loved most.

One day I ran into an acquaintance I hadn't seen since the crash.

Her reaction was "You're looking so good, Sandy! You've recovered so quickly!" She obviously thought I would be ready to return to work any day.

When I got home after that encounter, I walked into the bathroom and studied myself in the mirror. It might have been easier to accept if the features of my face had been burned off or if I'd have lost an arm or a leg. Instead, the image staring back at me from my mirror looked just fine, like the image I tried to project to the people around me. But it was a lie. And I hated that unscarred reflection in my mirror.

There, alone in that bathroom, I began to shout with frustration and claw at that lying, reflected face. I pounded the glass with my fists until it split and crashed to the floor, shattering into tiny shards. Then I fled to my room and sobbed for hours.

Lying across my bed, I thought about my friends and family members who'd tried to tell me, "You have to pick up the pieces and go on with your life, Sandy. You're young enough to start over. At least you're alive."

They couldn't understand that the Sandy Purl they knew really had died. They were left with a stranger. I was a stranger to myself—a stranger I didn't know and didn't like! Sure, I was lucky to be alive. I had no explanation other than luck. "But," I asked myself, "is it enough just to be alive?"

As time passed, with the encouragement of her therapist, and at the urging of friends and family, Sandy took a major step toward starting a new life. In September she rented an apartment of her own and immediately began to feel a new sense of control over her life.

But less than a month passed before another letter from Southern arrived at her new address. Her regular salary was to be terminated after October 5. Starting with the next pay period, she would go on worker's compensation.

This second letter wasn't as surprising as the first. But the timing couldn't have been worse. There was no way she could keep her apartment on $95 a week of worker's compensation.

Sandy quickly learned the company wasn't about to reconsider changing its mind again. As soon as Mike heard the news, he suggest-

ed Sandy might come back and live with him; maybe they could start over. She began to seriously consider the idea.

Around the first of October, I had to make the dreaded trip to Southern headquarters to do the paperwork to start my worker's compensation. Sitting in the accounting office, listening to one of the supervisors explain my options, I had to fight the urge to storm out and slam the door. Instead, I sat quietly and signed my name on a form requesting pay for all my accrued sick leave before worker's compensation would start.

When all the arrangements were done, I walked to my car as quickly as possible. I'd just backed out of my spot and started toward the exit when I saw Sam Brady walking across the parking lot. Without a second thought, I stomped on the gas and aimed my car right at him. As I sped through that parking lot who I saw was not just the vice-president of the company I felt had abandoned me; in that moment Sam Brady became the focus of all my pain, hatred, and frustration. With my foot pressing the floorboard, I knew this would be my revenge.

But something happened. Without making any conscious decision, I felt my foot hit the brake and heard my tires squeal. Brady turned suddenly and froze, his face registering shocked surprise as my car skidded to a halt right in front of him. I don't think he recognized me until he walked shakily to the side of my car and looked in. Then he exclaimed, "Sandy! Do you always drive like that?"

"Only on Fridays," I snapped. Then I squealed my tires and raced out of the parking lot.

The parking lot incident shook Sandy perhaps more than it had Brady. For after months of bitterness and angry threats, her feelings had almost burst through into actions. And it scared her. She would have gone to her therapist right away to talk about what had happened, but he was out of town at a psychology convention. Her next scheduled session was more than a week away.

During that week, Sandy became extremely ill with severe abdominal pain. Since she'd been having some physical problems with her menstrual periods since the crash, she went in to see her doctor. He

*listened to her tell about her symptoms, asked some questions, and fi-
nally said, "I'd like to run a routine pregnancy test on you."*

I was to check back the next day after the results came back
from the lab. I drove to my sister Sue's to be with my mother when
I made the call; I couldn't face the news alone.

I'd always loved kids. Wanted kids. But not now, not in the middle of everything else. Not only was I in no shape physically or
emotionally to be pregnant; I also knew the stess I'd been under
and the prescription drugs I'd been on posed serious threats to the
health of any fetus. So I sat at Sue's dining room table, trying to
psych myself up to dial my doctor's number, telling myself, "It's
impossible." First, I'd been using an IUD as birth control. And,
second, Mike and I had only attempted sex a couple times since
the crash. So how could I be pregnant?

Yet the moment the doctor had said, "pregnancy test," my in-
stantaneous thought had been "Oh, God, no! I'm pregnant!" I
knew it seemed impossible. But some inner sense told me it was
true.

I dialed the number. When the receptionist answered I gave my
name and told her why I was calling. She put me on hold for only
a few moments before coming back on the line to say the results
were positive and the doctor had made me an appointment with a
specialist the day after tomorrow. I wrote down the name and address of the other doctor and hung up. My mother came over to
me as I stared at the phone and put her arms around me. We cried
together.

*Sandy knew the impending appointment with the second doctor
would be to discuss the prospect of a therapeutic abortion. Her own
doctor had already explained that with her IUD in place, the fetus
would almost certainly be aborted naturally if the pregnancy was allowed to continue. And there was no way to remove the IUD without
taking the fetus. He also had told her continuing the pregnancy could
pose a serious threat to her own life.*

*Sandy felt like a helpless pawn, manipulated by circumstances that
allowed her no choices. With great relief, she remembered she had a
therapy session scheduled the very next morning. She needed to talk.*

My mind spun as I walked into the office building housing my therapist's office. So many things had happened I couldn't decide where I would start. I had to dump everything somewhere, on someone who would just listen. But when I reached the office, the door was locked.

After a few minutes of waiting, I headed for the building's snack bar to use the pay phone and dialed the therapist's home number.

The phone rang twice.

"Hello?"

"Why aren't you at the office? This is Sandy. We had an appointment, and I really have to talk to you."

"Dammit, Sandy, *I* don't want to talk to *you*!"

My arm holding the receiver went limp. It dropped a few inches away from my face as I mumbled, "Why?"

"The damned company you worked for never pays its bills. I don't work for free, you know," he retorted.

"Wait a minute. You knew from the beginning it would be a long time before the company settled with you. You, more than anyone, know how they've been about anything to do with money. Why are you bringing this up now?"

"There's something else," he admitted.

"What?"

"Don't you know?"

I waited quietly for him to continue. He didn't.

"I'm in no mood for guessing games."

"I'm in love with you."

"*What* did you say?" I whispered incredulously.

"I said, I need you! I want you. I don't what to be your doctor anymore. There's so much more to our relationship . . . "

"This is crazy. Stop! I'm going home." I hung the receiver firmly back on the cradle. The I ran out of that snack bar, down the hall, and out the door to my car.

All the way home I searched my memory. I'd been totally self-involved whenever I'd gone in for therapy; maybe there were clues I just hadn't picked up on, little signals I should have seen and realized the doctor's support and concern had become more than professional. But I could remember nothing to indicate that was true. By the time I reached my apartment, I'd convinced myself there had to be something else wrong. The guy's voice had sounded a little funny. Maybe he was on drugs or something. there had to be a logical explanation.

The phone rang as I walked into my apartment. I sat down on the end of my bed, took a deep breath, and lifted the receiver. "Sandy, I am serious. You are the most desirable woman I've ever met. I dream about you." His voice sounded like my doctor's, but this man went on and on in graphic detail, vividly describing his sick fantasies.

I hung up and began pacing the hardwood floor. "This isn't really happening. What's he trying to do to me?"

The phone rang again. I answered. He told me he knew I loved him, he'd known it since I first started coming to him. Exasperated, I leveled with him in the strongest voice I could muster, "Look, you've made a big mistake. I don't love you. I have never loved you. I came to you because I needed help. What are you trying to do to me?"

"You don't need my help," he soothed. "You'll be okay. You'll always be okay, Sandy. In fact, I've figured out why you lived through that plane crash." He paused, obviously baiting my curiosity. "You lived because you'd do anything to survive," he paused again, "including kill your own father!"

Gasping violently, I slammed the receiver down on the cradle.

A short while later the therapist called again. And then again a few minutes later. With each call he sounded less and less rational, and Sandy began to focus not on her own feelings of shock and repulsion, but on the obvious problems of the therapist. He seemed to be regressing verbally and mentally with each phone call, until he was talking like a preschooler and fantasizing about playing with Sandy in a sandbox.

Convinced by this stage that something was drastically wrong, Sandy felt certain he was on some kind of dangerous drug trip. So she called on a social worker friend to ask her advice. The woman heard the story and agreed the man needed some help. But when Sandy called the therapist's house to try to talk him into getting professional assistance, no one answered. He was gone.

Sandy spent the rest of the day by the phone, calling every few minutes in an attempt to reach the psychologist. It wasn't until late that night that a woman answered the man's phone. At first she wouldn't tell Sandy what was going on, but when Sandy informed her what had been happening all day and insisted on some sort of explanation, the woman relented. She said that while at a professional convention the week before, the therapist had taken part in some experimental role-playing exercises. The experience had triggered some problems he'd been struggling with personally for some time, and everything just came apart for him. Sandy found out later he had to be hospitalized that evening and later gave up his counseling career.

I went to bed numb and exhausted that night. But I couldn't sleep. I kept asking myself and the silent bedroom walls, "What else can happen? Can life ever be normal again?" Once again I had been betrayed. First my company deserted me. Now the one person who had heard my deepest despair had literally cracked.

But the walls stayed silent.

I'd never felt more alone than I did the next day when I went in to see the gynecological specialist. After a brief exam, he recommended the abortion. There seemed nothing to do but agree. He scheduled the procedure for two days later. I left to call Mike and break the news.

Mike couldn't have been more supportive. I'd never needed him more. He flew up from New Orleans the next day, and went with me to the clinic for the D-and-C. He sat in the waiting room while I went through the painful procedure. He heard the commotion, as did everyone in the clinic, that occurred in the recovery room, where I lost control and began screaming at the other women, "Grab your ankles. Bend down and grab your ankles."

As I walked out of that clinic under my own power a short while later, I wept from the physical pain. But even more I wept over the emotional loss of the baby I'd always wanted—wanted until April 4, 1977. When the thought struck me that the death toll for the crash had just increased to seventy-three, I cried some more and asked myself, "Will it never end? First there was Daddy. Then the crash. And now this. Why am I always the one who has to go on living?"

But Mike was with me again, and the tears we shared drew us closer than we'd been in months. It felt so right to be together that we decided we'd give our relationship another chance.

Thus, incredibly, right when things had seemed so dark, I saw a glimmer of hope.

Chapter 7

Within a week, Mike arranged for movers to pick up all my belongings and I moved out of my apartment. Mike went on to Denver, to begin a new job November 1 and to look for a place we could live there. I planned to stay with my sister Sue for a week or so and finish up any business in Atlanta.

One day before I left town, I drove out to the airport with a friend to meet another friend's flight. Waiting in the crew lounge, I noticed a Southern DC-9 at a gate. I don't know why—perhaps my courage was buoyed by my newfound optimism over my marriage and my impending move to Denver—but I turned to my friend Hazel and said, "I want to get on that airplane!"

Hazel immediately understood. "Okay," she said. "I'll wait here."

I walked through the door marked "Southern Airways," through the crew area, and onto the ramp. A couple of the ramp agents looked up, but they recognized me and just waved. Striding across that hundred-foot stretch of black asphalt, a little voice inside me screamed, "No! Stop!" But I kept my feet going. With the familiar smell of jet fuel and the whine of taxiing aircraft all around me, I could feel the inner tension build. But I didn't even hesitate when I reached the bottom of the steps; I climbed them quickly and deliberately, only pausing for a second at the top to take a deep breath before I stepped through the hatch into the plane.

First I turned to the left and looked into the empty cockpit. So far, so good. I saw only the usual black instrument panel filled with the same dials and gauges I'd seen thousands of times.

So I turned around and I looked back through the long empty tube of the cabin. But the seats weren't empty! Instead I saw row after row of faces, the faces of my passengers on Flight 242. They were looking at me just the way they had when I'd made the routine briefing before takeoff that day in Huntsville.

I screamed and ran out of the plane and down the steps. I didn't stop running until I reached the terminal building. When I burst into the crew lounge and Hazel threw her arms around me, every muscle in my body was shaking. All I could say for several minutes was "I did it. I did it." Despite the trauma, I felt I'd fought and won a major battle in the war against my memories.

For the next few days I couldn't seem to force that experience out of my mind for more than a few minutes at a time. It had been as if someone had taken a snapshot on the afternoon of April 4 and etched the photographic image into my memory. Looking into that empty cabin seven months later, I saw the faces of my passengers in such detail I could have picked them out of a group portrait.

During the time Sandy remained in Atlanta, she decided if she wasn't going to get a regular paycheck, she would at least send Southern's personnel department an itemized list of the belongings she had lost in the crash. She figured that the cash reimbursement for her clothes, jewelry, and other personal items lost in the crash could help her get by financially.

But some time later, Sandy got another response on official Southern letterhead saying the company had received her letter:

Perhaps you are not aware that we paid for three pairs of glasses . . . at a cost of $291.20. We have further paid personal expenses incurred by you, your relatives or friends, exclusive of medical benefits but including personal needs, in the amount of $2,174.71. Obviously, when you return to flying status, your uniform items will be replaced and, of course, your salary is continuing from your sick leave and workmen's compensation.

The letter concluded with an expression of concern that Sandy would continue progress to complete recovery and ended thus: "Please keep us advised of your status and let us know if there is anything else we can do to be of help to you."

Once more Sandy felt rejected by her company. Her admittedly paranoid feelings of harassment were reinforced by several calls from the same man in personnel who had sent the letter. Evidently angered by her request for reimbursement and distressed by a new, somewhat critical article in the Atlanta Constitution *about the October 5 cutoff of Sandy's pay, he would call a couple of times a week to demand of Sandy, "What do you want from us? What do you think you're going to get out of this?" Sandy finally stopped talking to him.*

After she had wrapped up her business in Atlanta, Sandy drove to Ft. Walton to meet a friend of hers and Mike's who'd volunteered to help drive to Denver. But by the time she reached Florida a cold she'd been fighting had progressed to strep and quickly deteriorated to the point a doctor prescribed antibiotics and ordered her to bed.

For the next two weeks, until she was well enough to travel, Sandy stayed with a cousin in Ft. Walton. She wrote Mike every day, and he wrote back. Their letters overflowed with dreams and promises about the way their future together would be. So each day her body grew stronger, her hope for a new, normal-again life also grew. Denver promised to be a fresh start for both Mike and Sandy. They'd be away from their families, old friends, Sandy's job, and their memories. They'd only have each other, but they both felt they could build the rest of their lives on the foundation of that relationship.

Our friend and I arrived in Denver early on Thanksgiving morning. I couldn't have been more thankful. I ran into Mike's arms and gave him a heartfelt, hope-filled embrace.

Mike volunteered to reward our friend's kindness with a holiday on the ski slopes. Since my back still gave me problems, I stayed home and worked around the new apartment. I guess reality first hit when I looked at the pile of boxes sitting in the middle of the living room floor. I'd packed them up and sent them off to my new life almost a month before. And here they were, the same cardboard boxes, filled with the same junk, the same old brown stoneware, the same wooden cannisters, waiting for the same Sandy to unpack them.

For a long time I sat alone in that living room, overwhelmed and paralyzed by the task I knew lay ahead. The past, like the ceiling-high pile of boxes, had moved to Denver with me and waited to be unpacked. And I couldn't do either alone. I needed Mike. Suddenly I realized the fantasy promises we'd made each other in our letters were going to be tough, if not impossible, to pull off in real life.

Instead of being together forever as we'd talked about in the letters we'd written, it seemed we were *never* together. His company had assigned Mike to a building project in Los Angeles. So he was gone all week, every week. When he got home on the weekend, he wanted to take full advantage of the early season skiing. We just weren't getting the time with each other we needed.

Instead of an exciting new life with my husband in Denver, I was alone in a city where I knew no one. My entire social life consisted of visits to the doctor three times a week, for physical therapy on my back. I'd go early so I could chat with the receptionist; I even went to lunch with her a couple of times.

By the time Mike got home on the weekend, I'd built up so much resentment and frustration that I didn't even want to see him. That chasm between us grew even greater when he began to suspect me of having an affair.

The first accusation came out of the blue. One day he arrived home to tell me a message for me had been relayed to his office (we were still waiting for a phone to be installed in our apartment) from a guy named Stan in Los Angeles. Mike demanded to know who Stan was and what he wanted.

I explained that I'd met Stan on a flight I'd worked only a week or so before the crash. He had told me he lived in Los Angeles, so I'd given him the name of an old high school girlfriend who lived there and told him he ought to give her a call and ask her out. He'd called Liz, and they'd gone out a couple of times. When he'd read about the crash in the papers, he'd called to see how I was doing. During the summer, he and Liz had each called to keep tabs on me.

He'd been passing through Atlanta early in October, and he'd asked me out to dinner so we could talk and he could take a full report on my progress back to Liz. So I'd gone. I'd told him at the time I was still struggling with whether or not Mike and I would ever get back together. He just listened and let me talk. I concluded my explanation to Mike by saying, "He's just a friend."

Mike wasn't convinced. In fact, he'd already called Stan back and told him off. And now he was accusing me of having an affair with Stan. He even asked me if the pregnancy had been Stan's baby. I tried to persuade Mike this was just a terrible misunderstanding. But before long, neither one of us was very rational. I finally stormed out of the room, but as I did, I could feel the last remnants of my Denver dream come crashing down.

I called Stan the next day to apologize for the situation he'd been put in. I learned that he'd called Atlanta to check up on me, and my sister had given him my cousin's number in Ft. Walton. By the time he reached her, I was gone, so she gave him Mike's office number. But knowing how the whole mixup had started didn't solve anything.

After that, Mike became truly obsessed with suspicion. He demanded I stop seeing the physical therapist three times a week. Arguing only seemed to confirm his suspicions. Whatever I said, I couldn't convince him that the physical distance in our own relationship wasn't because I was carrying on any other relationship. The problem wasn't another man any more than it was Mike. I didn't know how to explain what the problem was—I wasn't physically ready for love because I wasn't emotionally capable of love. I didn't even want to be touched by my husband.

The accusations, like the continuing physical abstinence, only intensified the long, lonely weeks. I knew the last few months had been hard on Mike; I wanted to be understanding. But I couldn't even understand myself.

I spent hours every day trying. All I had to do was clean house and think. Our apartment was soon in perfect order, and I wanted anyone who came in to think my life was the same way.

In my own mind, I still thought of my life as two distinct parts: before the crash and after the crash. They were like two jigsaw puzzles with the same picture, the same person in each one. The same prints taken from the same negative. But the two puzzles had been cut with a different punch. Someone had mixed up all the pieces and none of them were interchangeable. Maybe everything from my old life would have to go before I could get a new life together.

The marriage piece of my new life certainly wasn't working. I'd get so resentful when Mike was gone and so angry when he came home with his accusations that I began to avoid him. If I knew he was going to be around home, I'd go shopping or to a movie. He had his room, I had mine. We became roommates whose paths seldom crossed.

Almost every night the state of my marriage was driven home by a recurring nightmare: The smell of jet fuel and burning flesh fill the air. Smoldering, broken pieces of airplane surround me. I am frantically searching the wreckage for someone or something when I spot a char-black body lying on the ground. The head, neck, and shoulders are up off the ground; the back is arched. Arms and legs reach skyward as if straining to reach heaven. And that high-voltage power line lies right across the middle of the U-shaped corpse. I walk closer to the body, to try to determine whether it was male or female. It's so hard to tell that I bend closer to look for any remaining signs. As I study the charred featureless face, I clearly recognize it: it's Mike. And my own screams wake me up.

Night after night, time after time, the dream was the same. Each time I awakened shaking and soaked with sweat. I told myself it was only a nightmare. But it didn't take an expert to interpret those dreams. I had only to roll over and feel the cool sheets of my empty bed to realize I really *had* lost my husband in the crash of Flight 242.

The Sunday before Christmas, when I decided to go to church, Mike said he'd go with me. I hadn't gone often in the four years we'd lived together; this was the first time Mike ever went with me.

We slipped into the sanctuary and found a place in one of the back pews. But even listening to the organ prelude, I was asking myself why I'd come. The only answer I could think of was "It's almost Christmas, and going to church just seems like the natural thing to do." Before the service ever really began, I knew I'd made a mistake. The moment the congregation joined in the opening hymn, I began to weep.

When I looked around at all those good people around me, I couldn't help wondering how their lives compared to mine. I felt so out of place in that church service, so guilty for losing control of my life, so selfish and cruel for what I'd been putting my family and friends, especially Mike, through. I cried off and on through the service, wiping my nose and trying to dab inconspicuously at my eyes in hopes anyone who noticed would think I had a little cold. At the start of the benediction, we escaped quickly out the back without speaking to anyone. And I went home feeling even worse for the experience and thinking, "Not even religion has any solution for my mess."

Sandy's general feelings of discontent about her marriage and her career spread to encompass her relationship with her legal advisors. For no more logical reason than the fact she'd seen (not read) a copy of F. Lee Bailey's book on another airline disaster, Cleared for the Approach, *she decided to drop her own lawyers and use instead the prestigious New York firm of the famous defense lawyer. A phone call to Bailey's office and a brief handwritten note to her counsel in Washington, and she had a new legal team. But the rest of Sandy's life was not so easily changed.*

Christmas Day came and went without a tree or a special meal. Mike gave Sandy an expensive necklace, but his generosity only upset her because they'd agreed they didn't have enough money to buy gifts for each other. Early Christmas morning, Mike left the apartment to go skiing; since it was a Sunday, Sandy decided to give church another try. Again she cried through the service, and left as soon as she could afterward. She spent the afternoon in her apartment, alone, thinking about her family and the happy Christmases of childhood. Mike returned later and left early the next morning for another week in Los Angeles.

On the morning of December 28, I awakened late, feeling strangely sluggish. As I wriggled and squirmed to escape the tight tangle of sheets and covers, evidence of another restless night, I forced my eyes open. The next second I sat bolt upright, wondering where I was and how I'd gotten into this strange bedroom. Then I recognized the light green walls and the second-hand furniture. Somehow I'd awakened in the bedroom of my upstairs neighbor. Thoroughly confused, I crawled out of bed and slowly staggered toward the door. I hung onto the doorframe for a moment, to gain some equilibrium and then plodded down the hall to the living room.

Laura sat on her couch reading a newspaper and drinking coffee as I blundered into the room. She looked up, her dark, pert face clearly reflecting some of the bewilderment on my own face.

"Are you okay, Sandy?"

"I don't know. What am I doing here?"

She looked worried. "Don't you remember what happened last night?" she asked.

I shook my head.

So she told me the story. She'd gone out to walk her golden retriever late in the evening. The dog had run over near my bedroom window and started whining. When she'd gone to get him away from the building, Laura had heard me screaming and crying. She saw me lying on the floor just inside the big sliding glass doors to the patio, and heard me calling, "Help me, please help me!"

She'd talked me into opening the door for her, but she couldn't seem to break through my hysteria to get me to tell her what was wrong. So she'd loaded me in her compact car and driven me to the hospital.

Laura told me I'd screamed incoherently and wrestled with the attendants who had tried to subdue me. A doctor had finally sedated me and sent me home to get a good night's sleep.

"So I put you to bed up here where I could keep an eye on you," Laura finished.

She handed me a copy of the hospital report. I read,

Patient seen in emergency room in extreme anxiety state. Dreams relative to past airline crash in which she was a stewardess. Hysterical and in state of extreme emotional distress. Vistaril, 75 milligrams; Haldol, 2.5 milligrams. Home to follow up in the A.M.

I didn't remember any of it.

Within a few days, some things did seem to fall into place for Sandy. When her physical therapist's receptionist suddenly left the job, the doctor called Sandy and asked if she could fill in until he could find someone else. The job proved to be just what Sandy needed, and vice versa: Working long hours every day and extra time on the weekend, Sandy soon had the office organized more efficiently than it had ever been. Her new employer's appreciation and praise gave a big boost to her nearly nonexistent self-esteem.

Working in a doctor's office resurrected those teenage dreams of a career in the medical field. Sandy checked around and enrolled in a medical assistantship training program, scheduled to start on January 23. Slowly, one piece of the new puzzle was fitting in.

Taking the job did two things I would have thought were impossible. One, it opened a door of hope—a door through which I could see the promise of a normal future. And two, it made the situation between Mike and me even worse. He was convinced I was having an affair with the doctor, and no amount of denial would convince him. Not only did his accusations disturb me, but I also couldn't bear to watch his growing depression and his lack of appetite. When he came home after his first full work week in January, I confronted him.

"I can't take it anymore," I told him. "I want out. I want a divorce."

He argued, but I wouldn't budge. Together we went to an office supply store to pick up the legal forms we'd need to file for divorce on our own. Clinging like a newlywed to Mike's arm as we searched up and down the aisles for the right papers, I remember telling myself, "This is stupid!" I'd made up my mind, and I wasn't going to change it. Yet I couldn't let go of his arm.

Even after we brought the papers home, Mike tried to talk me out of it. He begged me to come to Los Angeles and stay with him during the weeks. But I couldn't do that: I had a job and planned to start back to school.

A week and a half passed before I finally nagged Mike into filling out his part of the papers. On January 16, we went together to file for our divorce. Walking up those long steps of the Denver County Courthouse, I held tightly to Mike's arm. When it was done, we descended those same steps—again, arm in arm!

Back at the apartment, I stood for a while in the doorway of Mike's bedroom and watched him pack up his clothes. The pain I felt caught me off guard. After all we'd been through, after all we'd lost, my feelings for Mike remained surprisingly strong. Convinced that I couldn't deal with those feelings until I got the rest of my life together, I fled to my own room until Mike had packed his suitcase and left.

A few days later, I walked into my apartment after work to discover that Mike had cleared out all his personal belongings. His stereo was gone, his closet completely bare. He'd left nearly all the furniture, yet the apartment seemed strangely empty. "This is what you wanted," I told myself.

"But," I countered, "I didn't have any choice."

Sandy soon found a roommate, a girl named Shannon, who was in the medical assistant's program Sandy had signed up for. When school started, Sandy threw all her energy into making a new life. Realizing immediately how much she'd lost in terms of study habits, Sandy told the doctor she worked for that she'd have to quit her job. But after helping him screen and hire her replacement, she agreed to work part-time as needed.

School quickly consumed her. After so many years out of the classroom, reading seemed like heavy labor. Sandy was regularly up until 2 and 3 A.M. studying. The material fascinated her, and her obvious aptitude in the medical field confirmed the new direction she'd chosen for her future.

For the first two weeks of school, Mike left me completely alone. I guess he thought he'd give me time to change my mind. When I didn't, he began calling just to talk. And just hearing his voice on the phone unleashed a surge of old feelings.

I went out with Mike for dinner on Valentine's Day. And again on our anniversary the week after that. He tried to talk me into stopping the divorce before the mandatory ninety days were up. But I still refused.

He began to act more and more desperate. Sometimes he followed me when I went places with friends from school. Mike started taking antidepressants and soon looked as if he'd lost twenty pounds or more.

I tried to get him to quit calling me. I said anything and everything I could think of to discourage any hope he might still have. When nothing else worked, I told him to leave me alone because I wanted to see other men. I recognized the irony of the lie even as I told it. Here I as trying to hurt Mike so he'd quit calling and then I wouldn't have to hurt him anymore!

It didn't work.

Again and again he'd call to ask, "What can I do, Sandy?" And again and again I'd cry and say, "I don't know. I don't know. I don't know," over and over.

The more he'd call, the more I felt he was trying to force a decision from me. I didn't think I could face one more forced decision. Circumstances had forced me to come to Denver, to choose a new career, to choose a divorce, to choose to go to school. I wouldn't be forced into another decision. So I quit taking Mike's calls.

In her renewed intent to make a clean break from Mike, Sandy tried to separate herself completely from her past. She soon earned a new role and reputation as an A student among her classmates at school. If anyone asked about her background, she told them she'd been a baby photographer (the job she had during and right after high school). She completely omitted any reference to work with the airlines. Only her roommate, Shannon, and Mary, another friend from school, knew a little of her story.

I still had terrible nightmares. Often I'd awaken rolling around on the floor with a mattress and screaming, "Grab your ankles." So I had to explain a little to Shannon. And since Mary often stayed over at our apartment to study, I had to tell her, too.

One day I was sitting in the living room of our apartment, watching television and brushing my hair. When I finished, I cleaned the brush and absentmindedly put the wad of hair in an ashtray on the end table. Later, as we were all sitting around studying, Mary lit up a cigarette, took a couple of puffs, and set it on the edge of the ashtray. The burning end of the cigarette ignited the hair; the scent of burning human hair instantaneously triggered my gag reflex and I vomited half-way across the living room. When my heaves finally subsided, I explained what had happened, apologized, and quickly cleaned up the mess.

Yet even though I couldn't completely forget the past, I was able to enjoy the present. Once I relearned forgotten study habits, school was fun and challenging. It filled my time and my mind. As I looked ahead toward completion of my medical assistant's certificate, I spent less and less time looking back.

On April 18, the day the divorce would be final, I attended class, just as I did every weekday. So this time Mike went to the courthouse by himself. I was in class when a message came from the dean's office that someone had come to see me and I left class and walked down to the lobby. It was Mike.

"I brought you the papers to sign to change back to your maiden name," he said as he held them out.

"Okay." I glanced over them quickly, signed them right there in the lobby against the wall, and handed them back. "That's it?"

"I guess so," he said. "Goodbye."

"Goodbye." As I stood and watched him walk through the front door, down the steps and out the walk, I wished I could feel something. Anger, sadness, grief. Anything would have been better than the "nothing" sensation that filled me.

Mike returned to Ft. Walton almost immediately after the divorce. Two days after Mike left town, however, I just *had* to talk to him. I didn't have a number for him in Ft. Walton, so I called him person to person at his parents. He wasn't there. And I heard his mother angrily yelling at the operator to tell me never to call there again. The operator tried to explain that the call wasn't collect, but Mike's mother said she'd refuse it anyway.

I hung up.

As I sat staring at the phone, the truth dawned on me: I'd divorced my husband. I'd cut myself off from the only man I loved.

My roomates couldn't understand what was going on. For weeks I'd done everything to avoid him. And now I was desolate because I couldn't talk to him.

I took the phone and locked myself in the closet of my bedroom where no one could see or hear me. I spent all afternoon calling number after number in Ft. Walton, trying to reach him. Countless times I rang Mike's parents, only to hang up the second his mother's voice sounded over the line. Finally, after I'd spent hours in the dark closet, Mike answered his parents' phone.

All I could do for several minutes was cry. When I composed myself enough to explain what had happened, Mike promised he'd always be willing to talk to me when I needed to talk. But he said he wouldn't come back to Denver. I was on my own.

When our conversation ended and I hung up, I slumped against the wall of the closet among the clothes, and shoes. The thought of a life without the man I had just divorced scared the hell out of me.

When I finally emerged from the closet, the night was dark. And the future I'd been focusing on for three months didn't look as bright, either.

Chapter 8

With Mike gone, Sandy threw every bit of energy into studying for her finals. During the next four weeks, she not only completed her term with straight A marks, but she also discovered the emotional strength to make a crucial decision regarding her future.

She knew she could wrap up the final term of her medical assistant program if she'd stay in Denver until fall. But there no longer seemed to be anything or anyone tying her to Denver. Her family was in Atlanta, so she decided she'd go back home to start over. Her success in school had convinced her life still held some good new options for her, and it also had renewed her self-confidence. Sandy told herself if determination and perseverance could make her an A student, then the same kind of effort would enable her to fly again. She felt she needed to give it a try before she went on with some other career.

Not even a mandatory communication with Southern Airways could curb my newfound optimism. In the cursory note I sent my New Orleans supervisor in May to ask for a second extension of my medical leave (I was now certain this would be my last such request), I wrote,

Louise,
Attached is a doctor's note required for another extension on my leave of absence. I am doing wonderful and I'm really looking forward to my return to flying real soon. Tell everyone I said, "Hi."

When Southern had received the first required note from my doctor and my first official request for a medical leave, a Southern executive had sent me a another disturbing letter, which said, in part,

Based on the circumstances of your case and in accordance with the Flight Attendant contract, a medical leave is granted for 90 days effective March 1, 1978.
Sandy, we do hope you will be able to return to work very soon. In the

interim, however, let me explain a few of our health benefits that may affect you. During a leave of absence, the employee's medical and dental health insurance is continued for 90 days without cost to the employee. After 90 days, the employee must pay the monthly premiums and arrangements must be made in advance. . . . Should you have any questions concerning your particular situation, please contact Employee Benefits, Southern Airways, Inc.

As part of our procedures for any employee on a medical leave, a doctor's release will be required prior to your returning to work. Additionally, a request for extension of your leave of absence must be received prior to the expiration of your current leave. If we have not heard from you concerning your intentions prior to May 29, 1978, we will assume you have elected to resign your position with Southern.

We're looking forward to your return. If we can be of any assistance, please let us know.

I'd been so upset when I opened that letter that I'd thrown and shattered a coffee cup against the wall and stomped about the apartment swearing at Southern's continuing "persecution" of me. But by renewal time in May, resolved that I'd have to start paying my own medical insurance premiums the first of June, I figured the problem would be taken care of as soon as I got back to Atlanta and resumed work.

In the meantime, I had some time to kill. Knowing that my new medical leave would extend till late in the summer, I determined to reward myself with my first real fun and relaxation since the crash. After Mike left Denver, Stan had called to invite me out to Los Angeles for a weekend with him at a posh resort in La Costa. I decided to go.

On May 12 my friends Mary and Shannon drove me to Denver's Stapleton International Airport, and I boarded a jet for my first flight in thirteen months. I'd bolstered my confidence with two valiums and a couple of cocktails; I was so numbed I recall nothing about the flight but a sort of subconscious terror. I do remember the relief that flooded over me as I ran off the plane, ecstatic that I'd finally climbed back up on the horse. Convinced that each flight would get easier, I felt more confident than ever I'd be back to work in no time.

When Sandy arrived in Los Angeles, she had no intention of begin-
ning a serious relationship with Stan. But the resort weekend made
her feel like a woman, like a desirable human being again. When Stan
invited her to come and stay with him for a while in Los Angeles, the
weekend stretched into a week, then two. Those days provided a most
peaceful diversion from her past troubles.

Each morning Stan would leave for his job as an account executive
with an advertising agency, leaving Sandy to herself. She'd retreat to
the roof of the apartment building for a morning of light reading and
sleep in the sunshine. When he came back at noon, she'd have lunch
made, and then she'd go back to the rooftop for the afternoon. Stan
would come home from work and they'd enjoy a leisurely evening din-
ner, watch some TV, and go to bed.

Stan seemed to be the perfect friend, listening, accepting her, apply-
ing no pressure. When she cried out in the night or woke up screaming
from one of her regular nightmares about the crash, he'd hold her and
ask if she wanted to talk about it. And as Sandy slowly began to relax
into the regular daily routine, the past faded farther and farther away.

I did nothing and saw no one but Stan for several days. And for
the first time in over a year I felt contented.

Then one afternoon, almost two weeks after I arrived in Los Angeles, I had spread a blanket and sheet out on the warm rooftop
and just sat down to absorb the view of Westwood and downtown
Los Angeles beyond, when I noticed another woman walking toward me across the roof. She was the first person I'd seen on that
roof. Wearing a swimsuit and carrying a blanket under her arm,
she obviously planned to share the sunshine with me.

We exchanged hellos, and she spread her blanket near mine. As
she sat down she sighed and said, "I'm bushed. I just flew back
from emergency training up in San Francisco, and all I want to do
is sleep."

"You fly?" I asked.

"I'm a flight attendant for United."

I didn't comment on that. We chit-chatted for a few minutes. I
learned her name was Cheryl. When she asked if I was new to the

apartment, I told her I was visiting Stan, that I'd been living in Denver and would be moving home to Atlanta in a few weeks.

"You're from Georgia?" she asked. "You don't sound southern."

"Well," I explained. "When I started to fly, I had to practice making announcements over the PA until I got rid of most of my accent."

Cheryl sat up and looked at me. "You fly?"

"I used to," I said, planning to let the conversation drop at that.

"Who with?"

"I flew for four years with Southern Airways."

"No kidding! We studied that Southern crash in our emergency training just this week. Saw the photos, listened to the tapes. I have to tell you, that Sandy was really something!"

An instant chill penetrated clear to my soul as I sat under a blazing sun on that Southern California rooftop. I looked over at Cheryl and I said stiffly, "You're not going to believe this. But I'm that Sandy."

And I watched Cheryl turn white as a sheet. I saw her hands begin to shake. I think we both felt something stronger than coincidence on that rooftop; I know I did.

Here I was, all alone on a deserted rooftop, 2,000 miles from home. In just over one year I'd lived in five different states, running from everyone and everything that had to do with that plane crash. Just when I thought I found my peace, a perfect stranger who had just studied the pictures of the crash and listened to the cockpit tapes of my instructions to my passengers walks up to me out of the blue and says, "That Sandy was really something."

When both of us regained control of our emotions we began to talk. Cheryl hesitantly asked a couple of questions about the crash. I could tell she was trying to judge how much I wanted to talk, so I openly admitted I still suffered from the emotional trauma. I kept most of the crash-related discussion focused on my feelings about Southern's lack of support.

As an example, I told her about my most recent correspondence from Southern. After I'd gotten the letter saying my insurance benefits would come to an end after ninety days on medical leave, Mike had written a letter on my behalf to Henry Byrd, president of the airlines, just a couple weeks before the divorce came through. Mike had reminded him of my devotion to duty and had listed a number of incidents he felt showed Southern's disregard for me and my emotional reaction to the crash. He had also protested the cutting off of insurance benefits, told how I felt abandoned by my company, and asked for some statement as to what position Southern Airways intended to take toward me and my future.

Over three weeks later, not long before I'd left Denver, a letter came to my apartment for Mike from Mr. Byrd. It said,

Dear Sir:

Your letter dated March 28, 1978 has been received and while I disagree with most of the statements made in your letter concerning Southern Airways and its personnel, I see no useful purpose to be served in debating with you.

My understanding is that Sandy is represented by counsel and I note that a copy of your letter was sent to an attorney.

I think that Southern's position has been fully set forth to [your wife].

That was it. A personal appeal for compassion and concern to the very top of the corporation, and the only response was, "I see no useful purpose to be served in debating with you." And that pretty clearly summarized the year-long attitude on the part of Southern.

Sandy's bitterness showed as she talked. Cheryl seemed appalled at Southern and genuinely sympathetic to Sandy's plight. The two young women shared an immediate emotional bond. Sandy had made a new friend.

In the following days, Cheryl invited Sandy out a couple of times to shop or have lunch with other friends. Since those friends also were flight attendants, the subject of the crash quite naturally came up. Sandy accepted the inevitable questions and did her best to answer them while steering away from the most emotional issues. Even so, being once again known as "Sandy Purl, the flight attendant," and talking openly about the crash for the first time in months, brought many memories closer to the surface.

A short while after I arrived in Los Angeles, Stan and some people he knew began planning a one-week excursion down to Baja, California, and I agreed to go with them. The first week in June, I boarded an Aero-Mexico 727 with Stan and the rest of the group headed for Cabo San Lucas, and made my second postcrash flight. Without any drugs this time, I tensed up so on takeoff I thought I might have permanently scarred Stan's arm. But he kept patting my hand and saying, "You'll be okay, Sandy, you'll be okay." And I *was* okay—till we started to land.

Suddenly I was screaming in an empty plane. Everyone was gone. All the seats were empty. I was the only one there. And I was scared and screaming. And all alone. Except for Stan. "What is Stan doing sitting beside me in an empty plane?" I thought. "This is a dream!" I felt such relief I began to cry. Then Stan touched my arm, and I realized this was real. Stan was sitting beside me in an empty plane. The rest of the passengers had long since disembarked. The dream was over. And I kept crying. "It's okay," Stan tried to reassure me. "We're okay. But you just relived the whole crash."

We sat on that empty plane until I regained my composure. Then Stan gently took my arm and led me into the terminal.

Later I insisted Stan tell me everything that happened during my blackout. He described my hysteria in embarrassing detail. I remembered nothing. And for the entire week we spent in Baja I watched the other people in our group and tried to imagine what they thought about me, what they knew about my reaction that I didn't even remember. Naturally, Stan had explained my problem to them, and no one acted unfriendly toward me. But I felt like a freak on exhibit in a sideshow.

After Baja, Sandy stayed in Los Angeles with Stan for another week. Then, despite her growing affection for him, she flew back to Denver and began packing what remaining personal possessions would fit in her car for the drive back home to Atlanta. Her furniture, except her bed, and all but a few of her clothes, had been shipped to Florida with Mike's stuff before she'd gone to Los Angeles. Now anything that couldn't be crammed into her Opel she decided she'd sell.

My second day back in Denver, I'd just walked back into the apartment after carrying a box down to the car when my phone rang. It was my union representative.

"Sandy!" she exclaimed, "We've been trying to reach you for the last two weeks."

"I've been staying in Los Angeles with a friend."

"You need to come to Washington, D.C., right away. There's a joint international AFL-CIO union convention starting here tomorrow, and you're going to receive an award for heroism."

"I'm *what*?"

She quickly explained that our union, the Transport Workers Union, and the Amalgamated Transit Union, were holding joint legislative sessions in Washington. They wanted to honor Cathy, the other flight attendant on Flight 242, and me at a big general session on Wednesday.

I told her she'd have to get me a ticket from Denver to Washington to Atlanta and back to Denver. I'd promised my sister I'd be home the next Sunday for my nephew's christening, and I didn't plan to miss that, award or no award. I'd have to come back to Denver after that and get my stuff and then move home. The union rep said she'd clear it and the next morning I took a first-class seat and braced myself for the takeoff of my flight to Washington.

When an off-duty (but uniformed) United flight attendant sat down next to me and introduced herself, I knew I would probably have to explain the reactions I expected on the flight. Indeed, just the obvious tension I suffered on the short taxi to the end of the runway prompted her to ask, "Are you okay? Can I do something to help?"

I told her who I was. She remembered the crash. She took my hand and talked to me during takeoff. Even so, I thought I'd crack the armrest as the plane lifted off the runway. But neither my deathgrip on the seat nor the flight attendant's attempt at distracting conversation could prevent my violent fit of shakes, which only slowly receded long after we reached cruising altitude. An internal tornado tied up my guts in knots, making breathing difficult for the entire flight.

During the trip I told my new friend some about Southern's official reaction to the crash and summarized my own problems. She gave me the name of a woman she knew, Del Mott, head of safety with the Association of Flight Attendants union, who was working with crash victims and their families. I put the slip of paper with Del Mott's name on it in my billfold, and landed in Washington with an encouragingly mild reaction.

The week in Washington turned out to be a disturbing combination of treat and torture for Sandy. She was joyously reunited with flight attendant friends who had stayed with her at Georgia Baptist Hospital after the crash. She even got to room with a good friend from Ft. Walton whom she hadn't seen in over a year. They had much personal news to catch up on and a lot of memories to relive.

The hardest part of the week was encountering Cathy again. Sandy wanted to embrace her when they met, but Cathy backed away. When Sandy asked if they could talk, Cathy said, "I don't want to talk with you. And I won't talk with you!

Cathy's reaction hit Sandy like a slap in the face. She saw it not as Cathy's unwillingness and inability to deal with the pain and memories of the crash, but as one more personal rejection.

The most positive experience of the week turned out to be the awards presentation. I sat with representatives of my flight attendants union in the back corner of the huge, smoke-clouded hotel ballroom. The vast majority of union members, elected representatives from bus, railroad, and airline worker locals around the country and the world, were men.

The executive vice-president of the international Transport Workers Union stepped to the podium at the front of the hall. And the next thing I knew he was talking about "a great tragedy in Georgia where seventy-two people died in a plane crash." He went on to say the union wanted to honor two of its members who had not only survived that tragic crash but who had performed their jobs heroically in the process.

When I heard my name called along with Cathy's, I stood quickly and wound my way through the tables to the front of the room. And as we stood in front of that crowd, the union executive read the inscription on our plaques. Mine said,

FLIGHT ATTENDANT SANDY PURL—COMMENDATION OF HEROISM

Presented to acknowledge competent and professional performance of duty aboard Southern Airways Flight 242, New Hope, Georgia, April 4, 1977. Your comprehensive emergency briefing of passengers in preparation for an emergency crash landing contributed to the number of survivors.

When he finished reading, he handed Cathy her plaque and me mine. Then he shook our hands and congratulated us, while cameras flashed and everyone applauded. Cathy stepped to the mike, said, "Thank you," and immediately turned to leave the dais. I stepped to the microphone feeling I had to say more.

I hadn't planned to make a speech. But I made one. I still don't know what I said, the words just poured out of me. When I asked my friends afterward they said I'd thanked the union for the award, summarized my experience, and talked about the importance of our jobs and the need to support each other. Whatever I said, it must have been good—I received a standing ovation.

The response prompted conflicting emotions. On the one hand, I didn't feel right accepting an award of heroism for just doing my job. Yet this was my first solely positive recognition for all I'd been through. A surge of pride coursed through me as I walked back to my table. I felt flattered by the award, and I knew I deserved it for my actions on April 4, 1977. But making my way through that ballroom, listening to the tribute of applause, and seeing the sympathetic tears rolling down the faces of many men throughout the audience, I couldn't help asking myself, "Where was the union's praise and support for the past fourteen months?"

On Saturday I met my lawyer for a short appointment, and he drove me to the airport to catch my flight to Atlanta. Everyone else had boarded, and the gate attendant was making the final boarding call, when I said goodbye and headed down the jetway to the plane. It wasn't until I stepped through the door, showed my boarding pass to the flight attendant and turned toward the cabin that I realized the plane was a DC-9, the same kind of plane that I had crashed in on April 4, 1977.

"No!" I stared in disbelief, turned, and bolted back up the

jetway to throw my arms around my very startled attorney, "It's a DC-9," I cried. "It's a DC-9."

The flight attendants came out to see what was wrong. Fortunately, one of them recognized me from the union convention and immediately realized what the problem was. But I still wouldn't get back on the plane. The captain came in to see what the holdup was. His crew members quickly filled him in, and he asked me, "Do you think you could ride in the cockpit?"

"I don't know," I responded. "I can try."

So the crew went back to the plane and opened the forward bathroom door so the other passengers wouldn't be watching and I wouldn't have to look back into the plane. Then they escorted me aboard and seated me (against all regulations) on the jumpseat just inside the cockpit. And that's where I stayed the entire flight.

The first person off the plane in Atlanta, I ran to the gate and fell into my mother's arms.

I'd survived a stress-filled week, and I was finally home in Atlanta in the bosom of my family.

Chapter 9

Unfortunately my welcome-home feelings didn't last long. By the time we reached the airport parking lot, my twin sister Candy began experiencing a strange numbness in her left leg. When she got home, she called her doctor, who diagnosed the problem as a potentially serious recurrence of an old back injury, and recommended hospitalization. So Candy spent the night of my homecoming in Georgia Baptist Hospital. And I spent the evening at my sister Sue's, reviewing one of the hardest weeks in my life. I cried myself to sleep that night, hurting not only for myself but also for my twin sister, the dearest, closest person to me in the whole world. My last waking thought was the question, "How much more can I take?"

I asked myself the same question the next day when I went to visit Candy in the hospital. When I got off the elevator on the fourth floor and headed for her room, I nearly panicked. I had suddenly realized Candy was not only in the same hospital I'd been in after the crash, but also she had been assigned to the same floor, the same ward, with the same nurses. She even had the same doctor.

Walking determinedly down the corridor looking for her room, I was afraid she'd even been given the same room. She hadn't, but her room *was* right next to the one I'd had. So when I strode in I tried to put on a cheerful face.

Not five minutes after I walked into the room, I told Candy, "I have to leave." Just that abruptly I turned and walked out of the room. I nearly broke into a run to reach the elevator. By the time the elevator doors opened again at the lobby, I was telling myself I couldn't go back.

When I regained control, however, I forced myself back on the elevator, through the orthopedics ward, and into her room once more. I lasted another five minutes before I had to get out. This time my shame was as strong as my emotional distress. My own sister was hurting. She needed me. And I still had too many problems to help her face hers.

Candy and I had always been close; we'd always been there for each other. I'd always taken the lead, being the stronger one in our relationship. Caring for Candy had been a lifelong duty. As a kid, whenever I'd saved my money to buy anything I'd save enough to buy two—one for Candy and one for me. In high school, I'd paid for her cheerleading outfits out of the earnings from my part-time job. I'd used my earnings to help pay her way to cheerleading camp when our parents couldn't afford it. Right or wrong, realistic or not, I'd always seen Candy as one of my responsibilities in life.

Now Candy was hurting. She needed me, and I couldn't bear to even sit in that room with her for more than five minutes at a time.

I'd found the answer to my question: "How much more can I take?" The answer was, "NO MORE!"

So when Stan called a couple of days later to say, "Sandy, I miss you. Come back and live with me," I saw the offer as the perfect escape. The past week had convinced me that the idea of going back on line with Southern was self-delusion. I was nowhere near ready to fly again, and probably never would be. Right then I wanted nothing more in the world than to be as far from Atlanta as I could get.

With Candy still in the hospital, I flew to Denver, packed my car, and drove nonstop to Los Angeles the next day. And I moved in with Stan, the one person in the world who had seen me at my worst and still wanted me.

But Los Angeles no longer provided the peace and refuge it had the first time for Sandy.

The dreams were worse than ever. Or rather my reactions to the dreams were worse than ever. I'd be sitting in bed screaming "Grab your ankles, grab your ankles" when I'd feel Stan reach over and shake me, saying, "It's okay, Sandy, it's just a dream." And I'd know it *was* okay; it was just a dream. But real adrenaline would be pumping through my body, and I'd keep right on feeling genuine terror and horror for an hour or two after Stan had rolled over and gone back to sleep.

The old dream of the char-broiled body with Mike's face on it was one of the regulars. Finding the bodies of the crew and being dragged away from them was another. Many a night I'd awaken to the sounds of my own screams and find myself desperately rubbing my hands across the sheets, trying to rid myself of the sensation of burned skin that had stuck to my hands as I'd pulled disembodied hands and arms out from under smoldering wreckage.

The nightmares became so vivid, and the nights so distressing, that I soon had to do something to keep control of my days. Hours alone in Stan's apartment, or sunning on the rooftop, no longer provided enough distraction to keep my mind preoccupied. I had my own car, so new options were open to me. I soon developed a daily pattern that worked—for a while, anyway.

I'd get up when Stan did, then soon after he left for his office, I'd put a cooler with a six-pack in my car and head for the beach. The sun and the surf always drew a crowd. A few beers would numb my memory just enough that I would feel like throwing a frisbee, playing a fierce game of basketball, and sometimes even laughing and talking with the other regulars, who soon became familiar faces.

When I began to run out of my own beer around noon every day, I'd begin drinking whatever was being passed around. Stan ate his lunches alone now. Around three o'clock every day I'd load my empty cooler in the car and head for home where I'd shower and be dressed before Stan returned from work. We'd share a couple of cocktails when he got home, then we'd drink wine with dinner. Most nights we'd have after-dinner drinks, and sometimes there'd be a little something more before bed.

For the next few weeks, Sandy's days were just as peaceful and carefree as they had been when she'd first arrived in Los Angeles back in May. From her breakfast beer to her scotch-and-water nightcap, she'd experience no flashbacks, no crying jags, and little or no memory of the past. Sandy's beach-and-booze strategy blocked it all out—until she tried to sleep. Then the lingering effects of the alcohol intensified all the pentup feelings and her reactions to them.

One night lightning flashed in my dream, and I suddenly awakened beside the bed, on the floor, holding a flickering lamp I'd knocked off the bedside table. I was screaming again: "Grab your ankles! Grab your ankles!"

I know that when I'd first come to Stan he thought, as I had thought, that the dreams would gradually go away. And in fact, before I'd gone to Washington, his compassion and acceptance had seemed to ease them. But now they were worse, with no sign of letting up. I could tell Stan was getting tired of it all, I could sense his building frustration. And I took his weariness over my problems as further evidence that I was now getting worse instead of better.

We were slowly but steadily drifting apart. Since I drank myself into a haze every day, I had nothing of interest to talk about when Stan got home from work. And his communication with me grew less and less as we spent most evenings drinking in silence and watching television. My problems were becoming too much for either of us to deal with. I felt that if I were going to keep Stan I'd have to shield him from any added strain.

Some nights I'd lie in the dark for hours, listening to the rhythmic breathing of the man sleeping beside me, holding my restless body as still as I could to keep him from waking. Whenever drowsiness crept too close, I'd threaten it with memories of past nightmares and promise, "Just a few more hours to morning." Sometimes I'd make it.

But the nightmares, the disrupted nights of sleep, and Sandy's deepening hysteria weren't the only stresses on her relationship with Stan. He had his own pressures and problems that summer.

Disgruntled with his job, he was seriously pondering an offer of another position with a different company. That would require a move to Salt Lake City. Moreover, his ex-wife was asking Stan to let their oldest boy live with him.

Stan couldn't seem to make up his mind about any of it. First he was going to take the new job; then he wasn't.

He seemed even more unsettled about his role as a father. At first he told his ex-wife he wouldn't take the older boy unless the other children came, too. There was talk about finding a big house in the country.

The idea of an instant family appealed to Sandy. She'd always wanted kids, and she felt an immediate bond with Stan's children from the moment she'd met them. Perhaps motherhood would prove to be the future she needed to replace the past. But no sooner did she begin daydreaming about big meals and PTA meetings than Stan decided he couldn't handle all three boys. Discussion of a condo with room just for the older boy (maybe) quickly replaced all talk of the house in the country. And if that didn't work out, after a few weeks the kid could go back to his mother or to a boarding school.

The most important criterion for any decision Stan faced seemed to be his own comfortable lifestyle. Anything that threatened that, a move to an unknown place or responsibilities as a father, posed a problem for Stan. And when I began to see this pattern in his attitude toward his own children, I had to ask myself, "Just where do I fit into his life, then? If he's not any more committed to his kids, how committed is he to me?"

The obvious answer to those questions seemed to leave me no alternative. Early in August I called Mike in Ft. Walton—the first contact we'd had in months. But just the familiar sound of his voice set my heart pounding and my hopes soaring. We'd hardly exchanged hellos before I plunged ahead with reckless abandon: "Mike, I'm so sorry. I still love you, and I want to be together again."

For a long time the receiver hung silent in my hand.

"Mike?"

Then his verdict. "It won't work, Sandy."

"Why? I still love you, Mike, more than anything. I know that now."

Silence. And finally, "It just won't work."

"Why? Is there someone else?"

More silence.

"Mike, are you seeing someone else?"

"Yes." That one word struck me with surprising pain.

"Is it someone I know?"

"Yes."

My first thought was "Not another flight attendant! That's all I need. Just one more way for all my old friends to find out how bad off I really am." I asked, "Well, who is it?"

At first the name didn't register. "Who?"

The second time it sank in. I knew the woman well.

By the time I hung up, I knew it was over with Mike forever. My alternatives were down to one.

I began to take more precautions than ever to hide my hysteria from Stan. After he'd drop to sleep at night, I'd slowly, carefully, quietly slip out of bed, and lie on the couch in the living room, as far from the bedroom as I could get.

The nightmares continued whenever I fell asleep. There was even a new dream. In it, one of my passengers refused to buckle up. So I picked up the loose seatbelt and began beating him and screaming and beating him until he died. I woke up crying and shouting over and over, "I didn't mean to kill him! I didn't mean to kill him!"

Sometimes my screaming didn't wake Stan. At least, he didn't always come out of the bedroom. Then one night I woke up rolling around on the living room floor, wrestling with the coffee table and screaming, "Cover him up. Please cover him up." As the image of the captain's face faded, I saw Stan standing over me and heard him saying, "Hold it down or you'll wake the neighbors."

In mid-August Stan decided to accept the new job. I flew with him to Salt Lake City for the weekend and watched him pick out a condo he liked. It had an extra bedroom for his oldest son in case the boarding school didn't work out. We returned immediately to Los Angeles with plans to make the move right after Labor Day. I still wasn't sure where I stood with Stan, but he seemed to assume I'd be going with him to Salt Lake City, and I didn't see any other option.

One day after work, driving over to his ex-wife's to pick up the boys for the evening, Stan mentioned he had an appointment the next day with Planned Parenthood.

"What for?" I asked.

"I'm thinking about getting a vasectomy."

"Wait a minute," I said. "Don't you think there are some implications to this that the two of us ought to talk about?"

"Why?"

His question brought an abrupt end to the conversation. But it forced an issue I knew I had to have settled.

The very next afternoon, as I fixed dinner, Stan walked into the kitchen. I took a deep breath and confronted him straight on: "Do you think you'll ever marry me?"

The way he responded told me far more than the answer itself. He didn't hem and haw. He didn't hesitate or pretend to give it any thought. He just said, "No," and walked out of the room.

Sometime later he asked me, "Are you still going with me to Salt Lake City?"

And I gave his question no more thought than he'd given mine. "Yes."

I reconsidered my answer countless times over the next couple weeks. I didn't want to go with Stan, but I was fresh out of options. The decision was set.

One day when I was alone and couldn't stop crying about the pointlessness of the upcoming move, I called Liz, my high school girlfriend that I'd put Stan in touch with when I'd first met him. But when I heard her voice, I couldn't choke out any words. All I could do was cry.

"Sandy? What's wrong?" she asked.

"I don't know," I finally choked out between sobs.

"What can I do to help?"

And again I could only whimper, "I don't know. I don't know."

Later I went over to Liz's. She was cleaning house, so I pitched in and cleaned furiously until there wasn't a speck of dirt anywhere in her apartment. As long as I could concentrate on some activity, I kept myself under control. But as soon as we stopped and plopped down on her couch to rest, the crying started. Liz put her arms around me and held me. Finally, when the tear ducts were empty and my insides ached from the wracking sobs, it all stopped as suddenly as it had started.

"I'm sorry, Liz," I said. "I don't ever know when the crying is going to start, and once it does I can't stop it. I don't know what to do." I told her about my dilemma with Stan. I told her I didn't want to go with him to Salt Lake, but he was the only security I had. "I don't know what to do," I concluded.

Liz reminded me of some of our times together during high school. She talked of the faith we'd professed and how she still found so much comfort in praying to God and reading her Bible. "Sandy," she said, "I think it's clear what you need to do. You need a strong point in your life right now, and I think you need to make God your strong point. Nothing less is going to help you."

I left Liz somewhat consoled but in no way convinced God had any answers for me. I thought back to the futility and discouragement I'd experienced at that church back in Denver. Religion had provided no solace then, and I was in much worse shape now.

Maybe it was because of the conviction in Liz's words, or perhaps it was sheer desperation, but for whatever reason, I went out soon after that to buy a Bible at a religious bookstore. As I waited at the cash register, one title in a rack of booklets caught my eye: "The Power of Positive Prayer." Liz had talked about prayer, but I didn't even know how to pray. So I picked up a copy, placed it on top of the Bible, and handed my purchases to the cashier.

As soon as I got back to Stan's apartment, I took the Bible out and sat down with it. Having no idea where to start, I opened it to the first book in the Old Testament and began to read from Genesis. "In the beginning God . . . "

And that's as far as I read before I blurted right out loud in that empty apartment, "But I'm not in the beginning. I'm in the *middle* of all this!" I closed the book and began to cry. God still couldn't help me.

By the day the movers arrived to pack all our stuff, I'd lost twenty pounds and had spent the better part of two long days sobbing myself sick. The packers were out on their break when I walked into the box-strewn living room. There, just inside the front window, in his uniform, with his jacket off as if he'd just walked out of the cockpit, just as I'd seen him alive for the last time, there, in

Stan's living room, stood Captain McKenzie. He smiled at me, and I heard him say, "I'm all right, Sandy."

The moment I heard the voice, I shrieked and threw myself on the floor and covered my face with my arm while I rolled back and forth. "I don't believe it! What's *happening* to me? I'm going crazy! I don't believe it," I shrieked.

Stan burst into the room, and I heard him shout, "What are you *doing*? Shut up!" But all I could do was cry, "Tell me he's gone, tell me he's gone!"

Stan scanned the room. "Who?"

"By the window. Captain McKenzie."

I saw a disgusted look cross Stan's face as he said curtly, "There's nothing there." It was as if he was asking, "What next?" His tone of voice, his whole attitude, seemed to imply I was seeing ghosts just to manipulate him or embarrass him in front of the neighbors.

I took the telephone and barricaded myself in the bathroom for the rest of the day. I called my mother three or four times, but all I could do was cry. For the past few months I'd been careful to call home only on my good days, when everything felt under control. So my hysteria caught my mother completely off guard. "You've always been so strong, Sandy. What's wrong?" she asked.

I could only blurt out my standard answer, "I don't know, Mama, I don't *know*!" How I hated those words. But they summed up my whole life.

Chapter 10

The morning after the movers left, Stan and I loaded the last of our personal belongings into the trunk of my Opel. I went back to check the apartment one last time. Walking slowly through the barren rooms, I couldn't help comparing their emptiness to mine. No warmth. No comfort. Only blank walls. I tried vainly to remember what had seemed so wonderful just three months before. Maybe it had all been an illusion.

When I got back out to the car and climbed in the passenger side, Stan backed out of the parking lot and we were on our way. Still there was no feeling of anticipation, no tinge of excitement about the coming changes in my life. I was going to Salt Lake City with Stan because there was no other direction to go.

By the time we reached the outskirts of Los Angeles, I'd raided the cooler for a breakfast beer. When we reached the desert, Stan joined me in another drink. A short while later we stopped for lunch, but I couldn't eat. So I pacified my stomach with another beer while Stan ate.

The longer we drove that day, the more trapped I felt. There was nothing for me in Salt Lake. No friends. No family. Only Stan. And he was little more than nothing now.

As the implications of this move began to sink in, the crying started again. I thought I heard Stan sigh in disgust at my first sobs. But when I glanced over at him, he sat statue-still, impassively glued to the steering wheel.

I wondered again why he put up with me. Maybe he had too much pity to kick me out. But he certainly didn't have enough compassion left to really care anymore. We were both drifting aimlessly, waiting for the other to make a decision to say, "No more."

"What is he getting out of this?" I asked myself. But I already knew the answer. He was getting me. A pretty face to be seen with. A housekeeper. A body, if not a spirit, to fulfill his desires.

The more I thought, the more it seemed he was taking everything and giving nothing. We were moving for his job, to his new condominium. We were leaving my friends in Los Angeles, and we were going in my car.

Suddenly I felt like a used and dirty whore. I had sold myself for a fleeting sense of security that had faded to nothing more than an empty relationship. I had spent everything and bought nothing.

The pervading hopelessness settled over me again, fueling my tears. The only sure way I could think of to stop them was to pop the top on another can and deliberately sip a beer. So I occupied the long hours of the drive alternately crying, drinking, and thinking.

We reached Las Vegas late that afternoon and found a motel at the edge of town. After taking a while to unwind, Stan decided we would check out the action at some of the casinos. We made a fast-food stop on our way to the Strip, but I didn't even order. "You'll waste away to nothing if you don't eat," Stan said half-heartedly. "What do you want?"

"Nothing," I insisted. And he gave up.

Las Vegas shone like a neon oasis in the desert night. And the day-bright glow lent a fantasy hue to the crowds of people who flowed from one casino to another, up and down the streets. But the lights and the life around me only magnified the deadness I felt inside.

Back at the motel, we caught the late night news before Stan announced he was going to bed. But when he headed into the suite's bedroom, I decided to spend the night on the couch. It was my most pointed concession yet to the growing disdain I felt for Stan. In as direct a way as I could handle right then, I was saying, "I don't want to be with you anymore."

When we pulled out of Las Vegas early the next morning, the night-time mirage of a vividly lighted oasis had become a pastel island of concrete in a sea of sand. The glitter had washed out in the glare of the Nevada sun. And ahead of me was another long, silent drive.

Once we did finally reach Salt Lake City, Stan wanted to go

straight to his new condominium. But I knew the movers wouldn't be there with the furniture yet, and I couldn't stand any more emptiness. What I didn't say was that I never wanted to move into that condo with Stan. I just insisted we find a motel.

Stan reluctantly agreed and checked us into the Salt Lake City Hilton, where we spent the longest weekend of my life. Stan had been distancing himself from me for some time, but now he seemed to deliberately withdraw what little he might have had left in our relationship. While I sat and cried and drank away the days, he totally ignored me, devoting his attention to football, baseball, and whatever else came on television. I spent my sleepless nights on the couch, crying off and on and despairing that my lonely hell would never end.

Sleep still hadn't claimed me when narrow shafts of Monday morning light began filtering in around the edges of the heavy motel-room curtains. I sat up and helplessly watched the inevitable happen as the furniture in the room took shape in the slowly receding darkness.

Stan's wake-up phone call finally rang with the suddenness of a judge's gavel, sentencing me to another one-day term. I rose and dressed because I had to; it was part of my prison routine.

When Stan came out of the bedroom dressed for his first day at his new job, I remembered I had reason to dread this morning. I was going to be alone in that motel room all day. The thought nearly petrified me.

"I have to have my car today," I told Stan. "I'm not going to be stuck by myself all day in this room."

The room service waiter knocked at the door before Stan could react to my ultimatum. He accepted the coffee and signed the check. When he returned with the coffee pot, I insisted again, "You can't use my car today."

"I don't need it," he replied. "I called for a rental. It'll be here any time."

I poured myself some coffee and sat down on the couch. Stan stood across the room sipping from his cup. Neither of us spoke again before he retreated to the bathroom to prepare to leave. I stared blankly at my coffee cup and slowly drained it. I didn't even respond to Stan's "I'll be back around six" as he closed the door on the way out.

All control deserted me the moment that door latched. I felt the hysteria build in my gut until the first sob erupted in my throat. I jumped to my feet and paced around the room.

I jerked open the curtains in front of the sliding doors, slid the panel aside, and stepped out on the balcony for a lungful of fresh air. Bracing myself against the railing, I looked down at the parking lot five floors below.

There was Stan, unlocking my car.

"He lied to me!" I thought. "*He is taking my car!*" And I started to scream down an angry curse. But just then he ducked back out of my car with a box, opened the door of the car next to mine, and put the box in it. Then he walked around to the back of my car, lifted the trunk, and began shifting its contents too, to the other car.

I stood transfixed on that balcony, like a spectator watching the final act of a drama. Stan's actions, his unloading of his stuff from my car, signaled the end. He was drawing the final curtain between us. The feeling had been gone for weeks. Now his actions said to me, "I'm not even going to use you anymore."

I stayed on that balcony until Stan's car pulled out of the parking lot and moved into the flow of traffic on the highway in front of the motel.

Around noon, when I thought I had gotten hold of myself, I splashed cold water on my face to try to get rid of the ugly red tear splotches and took a short walk around the motel. When I met anyone in the hall, I'd duck my head and look at the carpeting. Even then I was sure my swollen face and bloodshot eyes gave me away. But anything seemed better than the isolation of the room, so I forced myself to keep walking.

As I walked quickly thorugh the lobby and the desk clerk greeted me, I lost control again. Unable to mutter a response, I bit my lip and fled again to the sanctuary of my room. I was still there, sobbing away, when Stan returned that evening.

After another pointless visit to the hotel restaurant for supper and another evening of television, Stan flicked off the set at the end of the late news and went to bed.

Tuesday dawned. Another wake-up call set Stan in motion. I could hear him getting ready in the other room. When he came out, dressed for work, I was sitting up on the couch in my robe.

As we shared another silent breakfast of room service coffee, I just sat, watching him collect his papers and stuff them into his briefcase. When he had left, there didn't seem to be any point in getting dressed. So I just sat, my thoughts fogged with fatigue. My eyes burned. The muscles in my throat and chest ached from the hours of continuous, convulsive crying. After two weeks without being able to keep down a good solid meal, I felt too weak to go on. "I can't go on," I told myself. "Not like this."

What seemed like hours after Stan left, I mustered enough energy to get from the couch to the balcony. I stood with my hands gripping the railing and looked out at the mountains and bright blue sky. Then I looked down at the concrete below, and a cold chill came over me.

Standing there, staring down at the ground, I remembered something I'd seen in the newspaper a few weeks before—the story of a deranged mother who had thrown her five children off a motel balcony and then jumped herself. I stared down at that concrete and wondered, "What would it be like to jump? That mother died and escaped her problems. Maybe she wasn't so crazy."

Those thoughts scared me enough that I turned back around and looked back into the room. That's when I saw the knife Stan had left on the table just inside the door.

I went back in, walking past the table, and slumped back down on the couch. I was entranced with that knife. I couldn't take my eyes off it. Minutes passed before I realized I was crying again.

"I don't want to die," I argued with myself. "But I have to do something to make someone realize how sick I am. I need help!"

There was no one to help. I thought about the telephone. But I didn't know anyone in Salt Lake to call except Stan. And he couldn't help.

That's when I thought of the doctor I'd worked for in Denver.

"He will know what to do," I told myself as I grabbed for the phone.

I asked the operator to place the call collect. I no sooner heard the doctor accept the charges than I burst into blubbering hysteria.

"What's wrong, Sandy?" I heard the doctor ask.

But all I could get out was a garbled, "I'm sick. I'm so sick!"

The doctor waited until I began to regain a little control before he asked, "Are you in L.A.?"

"No. Salt Lake City."

"Where's Stan?"

"Gone," I said without explaining.

"Something wrong with your relationship?"

"Yeah," I answered before I blurted out a jumbled account of everything from the move to the thoughts on the balcony to the knife. I completed my report by telling the doctor I'd been crying for two straight days and pleading, "Tell me what to do. I'm so sick. Tell me what to do."

I don't know how much of my confused rambling he understood. When I stopped talking, I heard him calmly say, "Okay, Sandy. I want you to hang up, then call a cab and ask the driver to take you to the nearest hospital. When you get there, I want you to call me again. All right? Will you do that?"

"Okay," I said. "I will."

I hung up, automatically dressed, and packed a bag with pajamas and a change of clothes. For some unknown reason, I also threw in the Bible and the book on prayer I'd picked up at that Christian bookstore in Los Angeles.

Hurrying down to the parking lot, I climbed into my car and began driving before I realized I didn't even know where I was going. After two blocks, I spotted a gas station and pulled in to ask directions to the nearest hospital. The attendant told me where to turn. Five minutes later, I pulled into the Holy Cross Hospital parking lot. I slammed my car door shut and ran to the red arrows that led to the emergency entrance.

As I passed through the doors, the crying began again. But I also felt a tinge of hope. "Maybe, just maybe," I thought, "someone at this hospital can help."

Chapter 11

"What's wrong, dear?" a nurse asked, taking my arm before I'd gotten halfway across the emergency room lobby.

The moment she touched me, my teeth began to chatter and my whole body started trembling. I managed to babble a few choppy phrases: "Not my stomach . . . not head . . . crying two days . . . can't stop . . . need help . . . "

I don't know how much the nurse could decipher, but she put her arm around me and nodded. So I kept right on spilling the details. "Visiting town . . . staying motel . . . don't know anyone . . . plane crash . . . can't stop crying . . . need help . . . doctor in Denver . . . call him . . . he knows . . . he . . . "

"Okay, dear," the nurse interrupted. "I think I understand. If you'll just take a seat over there, I'll have a doctor here in a few minutes." She motioned to a row of seats across the lobby.

Already there were three people sitting in those chairs. And they were watching me. I clutched the nurse's arm as she turned to leave.

"I won't stay . . . if . . . if have to wait in here," I said, struggling to force the words out between the slowing sobs. "I just can't. Is . . . there somewhere I could . . . be alone? I could wait . . . in the ladies room?"

With that, the nurse led me to a small examination cubicle where I could wait in privacy. But a few minutes later, when a nun looked in on me, I begged her not to leave me by myself. So she stayed. She asked me a few questions, but when all I could do was cry and mumble, "I don't know," she just sat with her hand on my trembling arm. Together we waited.

Eventually, another nurse came and led me to a doctor's office. He asked what was wrong, and I told him the same things I'd told the first nurse. Maybe I was more coherent with him, or maybe he'd already talked with my doctor in Denver; I don't know. But he seemed to understand, nodding and jotting notes as I talked. When I finished, he said, "I'd like to keep you here for a little while until you can get things under control again. If that's okay with you, the nurse will take you upstairs to a room."

As I nodded, I felt a sense of relief flow through me. I was still scared and shaking, but I knew these people weren't going to let me hurt myself.

My shakes continued as I followed yet another nurse down the hall. By now my jaws ached from the violent chattering of my teeth. But the crying stopped as we got on the elevator. The nurse's presence reassured me.

The elevator doors slid open and we stepped out into a corridor. I balked when I saw the sign on the locked double doors: "Psychiatric Ward." But the nurse took my arm and led me along. She unlocked the doors, and we entered the ward. We stopped briefly at the nurse's station, where an on-duty nurse gave me a sedative. Then my escort said kindly, "Come on, Sandy. I'll show you to your room."

As we started down the hall, I noticed other patients. Some walked around in dazed circles, obviously drugged. Others leaned against the walls, staring blankly from glassy eyes. A few eyed me with curiosity, their faces creased with permanent, meaningless smiles.

Just the sight of those patients started me crying again.

I was forced to stop walking when an old woman stepped directly into my path. Like the others, she was dressed in ordinary street clothes. A large strand of her thin, white hair hung down in front of her right eye. I forced a smile for her through my sobs, but there was no response. She just stood there, wringing her hands and staring into my face.

I whirled around and confronted the nurse. "I can't stay! I don't belong here!"

"It's okay, Sandy," she said, understandingly. "We just want you to stay until we can help you over your crisis." And she led me around the old woman and on to my room.

Then, after showing me where everything was and suggesting I lie down and relax, the nurse left me to my thoughts and my tears.

Despite a sense of safety, I felt terribly out of place. "I'm not like all those other people out there," I told myself. "They're really sick."

I refused to believe I belonged in a mental ward. Yet I couldn't shake the nagging doubts about my own sanity—doubts that had plagued me ever since the crash. "The doctor did admit me without hesitation. Maybe I am worse off than I thought. I'm not any different from the others here in one way—I need someone to tell me what move to make next."

Then a terrifying thought hit me. "Maybe the tranquilizers turned those patients into zombies. Maybe it'll happen to me and I'll never get out."

"All the more reason to act as normal and controlled as possible," I told myself, trying to force a halt to the crying. And I did stop. I had my first chance to try out my "normal" act a few minutes later when an orderly in hospital greens came to take my temp and blood pressure.

"Hi," I greeted him, with a forced smile.

"How are you?" he asked.

"Much better now, thank you." I could say that with some conviction, because I always *was* much better when the crying stopped.

"Where you from?" he asked, as he wrapped my arm and pumped up the pressure.

"Well, I'm from Atlanta. But I live in Denver now. And I'm just passing through Salt Lake City. I'll only be here a day or so." I wanted to tell him I didn't belong there and hear him say he could tell. But that would have been too obvious. So instead, I wore my cheeriest mask and maintained a running conversation until he left the room.

I knew my act needed work.

Alone again, I decided to call Stan. "If he knows where I am, maybe he'll do something now."

When he finally answered, I said, "This is Sandy. I'm in the hospital."

"You're *what*?"

"I'm in the hospital," I repeated. "Holy Cross. Can you come?"

"I guess . . . sure," he said. "I'll be there as soon as I can."

It was almost noon. Assuming Stan would stop by on his lunch hour, I lay back down on the bed to wait.

A second orderly brought lunch and returned later to collect my untouched tray. Still Stan hadn't come.

I heard a bell, then a commotion in the corridor. A pretty nurse I hadn't seen yet stuck her head in the door and announced, "Exercise class—everyone out in the hall!"

Exercise sounded good to me. It would pass the time till Stan showed up. So I got up, put on my shoes, and after brushing my hair and splashing another cold-water treatment on my face, I stepped out of my room.

But I wasn't prepared for the sight that greeted me. A congregation of the most pathetic people I'd ever seen crowded that hospital hallway. Most of them stood like mannequins against the wall next to the doorways of their rooms as orderlies guided the last of the old ladies to their places in the long line that ran down both sides of the hall. When the man across from me met my eye and gave me a leering smile, I turned and fled into my room.

A nurse followed. "Please come out in the hall for exercise class," she insisted. "Everyone has to participate."

"I don't belong with those people," I argued. "I won't do anything till I see a doctor. And I'll walk out of this hospital before I go back out there."

Once she gave up and left, I threw myself on my bed and listened incredulously to the exercise class starting in the hall. One of the nurses called out instructions. "Open your eyes. Now close them. Raise your right hand," she coached. "Now put it down. Then your left hand . . . and down . . . now . . . "

I wanted to laugh. But instead I cried, saying over and over aloud to myself, "I'm not like those people. I don't really belong here. Somebody *please* tell me I don't belong here!"

Before long a nurse brought me another sedative. And I zonked out. When I awakened, my first thought was of Stan. Why wasn't he here? I looked at my watch. "Almost five o'clock," I thought. "Maybe he came and the nurses asked him to come back when I was awake. He'll be back soon."

An aide broke into my thoughts with a knock on the door before she carried my dinner tray into the room. She placed it in front of me and took the cover off the hot plate. But the aroma of food made me gag. The second she stepped out into the hall, I covered the plate again and shoved the tray away.

An hour later, I heard a man's footsteps coming down the hall and was certain it was Stan. I'd already jumped out of bed when a white-coated doctor carrying a clipboard stepped into the room. He greeted me and introduced himself. Then he asked me a few questions about myself, my feelings, and my dreams—questions that told me he already knew quite a bit.

After responding to a few of his queries, I asked the question that had been plaguing me ever since I walked into the ward. "I don't really belong here, do I, doctor?"

He shook his head. "No, you don't. But until you feel you can cope with your problems, this is a good place for you to stay. You shouldn't be afraid to stay."

"How long?" I wanted to know. "When will I be able to leave?"

"You can leave anytime you wish," he said. "You checked yourself in; you can check yourself out. Tonight, if you want. But I'd rather you stayed a little longer. I don't think there's anything you won't be able to handle. It's just a matter of you slowing down enough to deal with the problems you're going through right now." He smiled reassuringly. "The important thing for you to keep in mind is that you're going to be okay."

The rest of our conversation didn't register or really matter. All I could hear was the echo of those words: "You're going to be okay. You're going to be okay." I wanted to believe that so badly that by the time the doctor left, I'd psyched myself up enough to consider checking out that very night.

I was still thinking about leaving an hour later when a ward nurse came in to inform me, "You have a gentleman here to see you. You can talk to him in the lobby at the end of the hall."

"If he wants to see me, he can come to my room," I told her. I could feel the anger mounting inside. I thought it was about time Stan came to me instead of the other way around. And I wasn't going to hold a discussion with him in the lobby, with all those other patients staring and grinning at us.

The sight of Stan walking into the room was enough to burst the barrier holding my hostility inside. "Why didn't you come?" I demanded.

He looked puzzled. "I told you I'd be over later," he said.

"But it's seven o'clock! I thought you meant you'd be here as soon as you finished what you were working on right then."

When he didn't bother to respond with more than a shrug, it struck me that the doctors and nurses I'd met just that day showed more compassion and concern than did the man I'd lived with for four months. I'd finally reached the end of myself and checked into a mental ward, and he only came reluctantly, out of a sense of obligation.

There wasn't really anything to say—for either of us. Stan's attitude couldn't have been clearer if he'd spelled it out in giant letters on a billboard. It said, "What do you expect of me now? I've spent a whole summer with your hell. I didn't make you live with me. I didn't make you sleep with me. It was your choice. Just like this is your problem. Not mine."

The message was there. All over his face. In his downcast eyes. Stan just didn't have the guts to tell me outright.

Right there I made one of the most certain decisions in my life. "I'm staying in this hospital. I'm staying at least until the movers get here with my things. I will never spend another night with this man. It's over."

Despite my angry decision, I still had feelings for Stan. All day long I'd hoped that when he discovered how sick I was, he'd come and rescue me from the hospital and from myself. Now, as he stood, awkwardly, silently, in that hospital room, the hope died hard. Bitterness flooded into its place.

Even so, when Stan muttered something about having to leave and turned to go, relief tempered my anger. There was a finality to my feelings. I promised myself this was the last time Stan would see me emotionally distraught and turn his back to walk away.

Once Stan was gone, I tried to brace myself against the emotional aftershock that slowly set in by reminding myself of the doctor's words. "You're going to be okay." But after so many months of torment and struggle, optimism was hard to muster. Since I'd checked into the hospital, I felt closer to hope than I'd felt in months. But I still despaired that it was just out of my reach.

"The doctor says I'm going to be okay," I thought. "I should stay until I can handle this crisis. But what about when I leave? I need help. I can't take the doctor with me. I can't take the nurses. I won't take pills to keep myself under control. And I'll never take Stan.

"I can't even take the walls of the room to talk to. But I need someone to help me. I can't do it alone anymore. God, I need help."

"God?" At the thought of his name, I remembered Liz's advice back in Los Angeles: "You need to make something your strong point in life, Sandy. You can make God that strong point."

But I'd tried to talk to God before. Lots of times. I kept asking Him why He'd done all this to me. And He'd never answered.

Now, lying in that hospital bed, staring at the corner where the two walls met the ceiling, I tried again in desperation. "I can't go on, God. I've hurt long enough. I've cried until I can't cry anymore. I can't go on living like this. I need help and you're going to have to do something. I can't do it alone."

I still doubted my words were getting past the ceiling. "Maybe I'm not praying right."

That's when I remembered the books I'd stuck in my overnight bag. Since I'd tried the Bible before and gotten nowhere, I now pulled out "The Power of Positive Prayer" and started reading. It referred to the biblical book of James. So I thumbed hurriedly through the Bible, searching for the passage. When I finally found it, I read from the fourth chapter of James, which talks about conflicts and problems. Verses 9 and 10 said,

Let there be tears for the wrong things you have done. Let there be sorrow and sincere grief. Let there be sadness instead of laughter and gloom instead of joy. Then when you realize your worthlessness before the Lord, he will lift you up, encourage and help you.

Those verses hit me right where I was. I thought, "I have all those emotions, God. I feel that utter worthlessness. And I desperately need you to lift me up and encourage me. Please help, God."

For the next couple of hours, I cried and prayed and cried some more. But this crying was more than just empty spasms of despair. Now I cried real tears of relief and release as I poured out my fears, my emotions, and my sins. For the first time since the crash, I was letting everything go. "You'll just have to handle it, God," I prayed. "I can't do it anymore." Also, for the first time, I wasn't blaming Mike, Southern, or Stan for what had happened. I was the one who had run from everything and everyone, including him. I was the one, not God, who had strung out my problems over six states. It was I, not God, who had divorced Mike. And I was the one who had messed up my own life and hurt so many innocent people in the process.

At last I was willing to try to accept my responsibility, ask forgiveness, and face the past. As for the future, I prayed, "I need your help, God. I can't live my life on my own anymore."

Even as I prayed I knew I wouldn't have to face tomorrow alone. An overwhelming aura of peace filled the room. And filled me.

I fell into the deepest sleep I'd known for weeks.

Chapter 12

Sandy woke up the next morning feeling more rested than she'd felt in months. When the breakfast trays were delivered, she took hers down to the dayroom, along with most of the other patients on the ward, and ate the first complete, solid meal she'd been able to manage for days. After breakfast she played a couple of games of bumper pool and a few hands of cards with fellow patients before returning to the privacy of her room to rest.

Sandy spent much of the day alone, lying in bed, alternately praying and reading her book on prayer. A few times she wandered down to the dayroom to play games and talk. The staff psychiatrist stopped in for a brief chat and once again assured her she could leave whenever she wished. But the entire day proved such a relaxing, drastic change from any day in recent memory that Sandy decided to stay at least one more night. There wasn't anywhere else in Salt Lake City she wanted to stay.

The second morning I woke up in the hospital, I decided I at least owed Stan a phone call to let him know how much better I was doing. He listened noncommittally to my report and then informed me, "The packers just got here with all our stuff."

That news set my mind racing. I had one of the biggest decisions of my life to make. If all my personal belongings were here and waiting for me, there was no longer any reason to hang around Salt Lake City. My resolve never to go back to Stan hadn't weakened one bit. Yet I had no place to live, and almost no money. I began crossing off alternatives in my head even before I abruptly ended the conversation with the words, "I'll call you back when I decide what I'm going to do." I dropped the receiver on its cradle.

Within moments I was crying again, crying tears of frustration, loneliness, and uncertainty. I dialed my twin sister Candy. It took a while to get the story out between the sobs, but when I finally finished and told her, "I don't know what to do or where to go," Candy never hesitated a minute.

105

"Come home to us, Sandy," she said. "We've got an extra bed-room, and it'll be yours."

Candy didn't have to offer twice. I told her I'd be there as quick-ly as I could get back to Denver and clear up my leftover business there. I called Stan to say I was going home and I'd meet him a little later at the condo to get my stuff. I informed the hospital staff psychiatrist of my plans; he wrote me a two-week prescription of antidepressants to stabilize me until I could get home and settled. Then I checked myself out.

The movers were still unpacking the moving van when I got to Stan's new place. So I just moved most of my stuff right off the truck and into my car. Stan said he'd drive with me as far as Den-ver. Since I'd only had two decent nights' sleep in weeks and still didn't feel in the best of health, I accepted the offer without pro-test. Besides wanting the help, I felt my relationship with Stan needed to come to some better resolution than we'd had in the hospital. Because of his offer, I figured Stan must have felt the same way.

I figured wrong. I never did find out why Stan offered to go with me. Obligation? Guilt? There was certainly no attempt on either of our parts to settle anything. A brittle silence filled the car for al-most the entire 500-mile trip. We drove straight through, and I drove most of the way. The closer we came to Denver, the more frustrated and angry I became.

From time to time, I'd cast a furtive glance over at Stan's face, hoping to see some clue as to what had been so appealing to me just four months before. I sincerely wished I could dump him off somewhere in the remote Rockies, but I did the next best thing. When we finally arrived in Denver, I didn't even bother taking him by my old place. Instead, I went directly to the airport so he could catch the first flight back to Salt Lake. I didn't even park, I just followed the airport loop signs to the "Departing Passenger" area, wheeled the car into the curb between taxis, and waited for him to climb out.

"Well," he said. "Goodbye."

Perhaps I should have felt something. But I didn't. "Goodbye," was all I said before he got out. I waited a moment while he reached into the back for his bag. Then he closed the door. By the time he had crossed the walk and reached the terminal doors, I had pulled out into traffic and was gone. I didn't even look back.

Once I had Stan disposed of, I went directly to my old apartment, which I'd subleased to my friends Shannon and Mary, and began packing whatever remaining clothes and personal things I could fit in my car. Rifling quickly through a stack of mail, I spotted an envelope from the Association of Flight Attendants. Why would I be getting correspondence from the AFA? It was a union rival of my own TWU. I quickly slit the envelope, pulled out the letter, and began to read.

It was from the head of the AFA's safety department, Del Mott. She'd been given my name by the United flight attendant I'd sat with on the flight to Washington back in June. The flight attendant had told her about our conversation, about the emotional problems I struggled with and Southern's reaction to my case. And Del said she was just writing to let me know that even though I wasn't an AFA member, she'd be glad to do whatever she could to help. She said she'd had some experience with surviving flight attendants and she thought it would be helpful if I'd talk to one of them— someone who had been through a crash and could understand some of what I was going through. She gave me the name and number of a girl who'd been working a Mohawk Airlines flight that had gone down in upstate New York in 1972. And Del concluded the letter by saying once again that she would personally be glad to do whatever she could to help if I'd get in touch with her.

By the time I finished the letter, I was crying again. But these weren't my usual tears of despair. These tears flowed out of gratitude and happiness. Just when I took my first steps of faith, knowing I had to go back and face the past, uncertain about the future and still wondering if anyone could really understand and help me, here was this letter. It offered me the first promise of real understanding I'd felt since the day of the crash.

I checked the date at the top of the letter. It'd been written more than a month before. It had been sitting in my old apartment in

Denver, waiting for this moment. For me, as I reread Del's words, that letter was a sign from heaven. It was as if God were saying," You're going in the right direction. Whatever lies ahead, you can trust me. I'll provide whatever resources you need to go on." Again I felt the same peace that had blessed my psychiatric ward room in Salt Lake City.

That evening, just hours after I arrived back in Denver, I went to the graduation ceremonies for Mary and Shannon and the rest of the people with whom I'd started the medical assistantship program. Afterward, I finished packing the last of the odds and ends I could cram in my car. Next morning I took off for Atlanta, alone.

I've never had another trip like it, before or since. With every mile and town that rolled by, my excitement seemed to double. Though fully aware of all the uncertainties that lay ahead, I'd never felt happier. Hour after hour I talked aloud with God and with myself. For the first time in seventeen months—perhaps ever—I felt my life was coming under control.

I drove the first day until dusk. Then I pulled off the interstate in some little Missouri town and checked into a motel. When I finished registering in the lobby, I picked up a complimentary copy of *Reach Out*, the Living Bible paraphrase of the New Testament, and carried it off to my room.

Lying in that motel room bed, before I dropped off to sleep, I opened that *Reach Out* and began to read. What a wonderful discovery! Here was a Bible written in plain, straightforward English, unlike any I'd ever seen before. This too seemed a sign of God's grace to me. Less than a month before, in Los Angeles, I'd bought a Bible and closed it in confusion and despair after reading a single verse. Now passages practically jumped off each page—passages that encouraged and spoke to me and my situation. I read that *Reach Out* New Testament for hours, until my tired eyes could no longer focus on the blurry words and I fell soundly asleep.

The second day of the trip brought new terrain and even greater excitement. The closer I came to Atlanta, the greater my sense of elation and the louder I thanked God.

I stopped for gas and something to eat in an interstate truck stop somewhere in Tennessee. When I'd paid the cashier and headed out the door, she called after me, "God bless you!" I almost turned around and went back in to say, "He already has!" and tell her my whole story. Instead, I walked to the car and headed on down the road, fueled by one more encouraging sign that somehow everything was going to work out.

My watch showed almost 2 A.M. when I pulled in to Candy's darkened apartment complex. I couldn't see the building numbers clearly in the dark, so I cruised slowly through the parking lots until I spotted Candy's car. Minutes later I knocked on her door and heard the sound of footsteps coming inside. The deadbolt slid free, the door swung wide open, and Candy and I nearly hugged the stuffing out of each other. When we finally gained control of our happy tears, we stepped back and looked at each other. She worriedly nagged at how skinny and haggard I looked, and I cried to see her in a body brace designed to help correct her back problem.

Candy pulled me into the kitchen, where she put on a pot of coffee and sat me down at the table. We talked until dawn. Despite the exhaustion of my travel, I'd found a reserve of strength I hadn't felt in ages. I was finally home.

One evidence of Sandy's newfound strength came that very first morning back in Atlanta. After months of depending on lawyers and intermediaries to communicate with Southern Airways for her, Sandy made a personal phone call as soon as the offices opened. Intending to get the name of a company-approved therapist, she asked to speak to the head of flight attendant services. When a secretary said he was unavailable, Sandy left her name and a message that she needed to talk to him as soon as possible.

When he hadn't returned the call by three days later, Sandy called again. Told the official still wasn't available, Sandy informed the secretary, "I'm sick and I need a doctor right away. All I want is the name of a company-approved doctor so I can be sure the insurance will pay."

The secretary sent Sandy to the workers' compensation office where a man told Sandy her insurance would cover any qualified therapist

she wished to consult. Encouraged by the man's reassurance, Sandy
saw this flexibility as a major step forward in her relationship with the
airline. She promptly asked a social worker friend for a recommenda-
tion and made an appointment for the next day.

My mind raced faster than my car on the ten-minute drive to Dr.
Joseph Peek's office. Everything had happened so fast. A little
over a week before, I'd come completely unglued in that Salt Lake
City hotel room. I'd been in and out of a hospital mental ward,
encountered God in an incredible new way, made a cross-country
trip, and moved in with my sister in the city I'd been running from
for nearly a year and a half.

For the first time in recent memory, I felt ready and able to go
forward in life, whatever that entailed. The question I needed to
answer was "Who is Sandy Purl?" One Sandy Purl had lived for
twenty-four years before April 4, 1977. But another Sandy Purl
had walked out of the wreckage, and that Sandy was now only
seventeen months old. Which one was I? Or was I both?

From the moment I'd walked out of that mental ward, I had felt
an unexplainable confidence that I would find the right answers,
that there was indeed a future for me to look forward to. I also
knew that first I needed some professional help in tackling some
very basic questions.

As I parked my car, I couldn't help thinking about the bizarre
experience with my last therapist. That fiasco had spooked me off
therapy for almost a year. Only the strength I'd found in recent
days had given me the courage to make this appointment.

But the ghost of that other therapist wasn't my biggest concern
as I opened the door marked "Joseph Peek, Ph.D., Clinical Psychologist" and entered the waiting room. My greatest fear at the
moment was that this therapist, any therapist, was going to listen
to my story, and conclude I was ready to go with life. "If he sends
me back to work too soon," I thought, "I'll crack under the pressure. And if that happens, I know Southern will jump at the
chance to fire me."

So I walked into my first appointment determined not to hide a
thing. I wanted him to see the whole picture. I longed for some

words of encouragement, but at the same time I desperately wanted him to assure me that "Yes, the picture really is bad!"

Dr. Peek stood as I walked into his office and greeted me warmly. A pleasant-mannered, middle-aged man, he seemed likeable
enough. He wore a heathery sort of sweater and tie that seemed to
give him a nonthreatening, fatherly air. A very basic paneled office, a semicluttered desk top, a nondescript brown couch, and a
couple of stuffed chairs all combined to give the room a comfortable feel. I knew I could talk here, to this man.

*And talk Sandy did. In the next hour she unloaded as much of her
story as she could get through, stopping only sporadically to reign in
her emotions and work her way to the bottom of the counselor's box of
Kleenex. What Joseph Peek saw was a young woman in a volatile state
of acute anxiety. "The obvious first challenge," he says, "was to somehow slow her down enough so that she could maintain the emotional
control needed to function in social and family situations. We seemed
to find a strong mutual rapport right from the start; I think perhaps
Sandy saw me as a bit of a father figure. And I was encouraged to get
off to such a good, open start. But within two or three sessions with
Sandy, I began to realize the complexity of her problems, the various
levels of conflict. There was the crash and all the trauma tied to that.
Then there was the conflict between her and her employer and the accompanying feelings of betrayal, her intense search for personal identity, a lifelong pattern of running from problems, and strong emotions
of grief and loneliness over the breakup of her marriage. One of the
clinical measurements I used, a basic Rorshach test, indicated a lot of
denial and hostility. So there was plenty for us to work through."*

*Though Sandy came away from their three-times-a-week sessions
encouraged by how many issues came out in the open, the growing
realization of how far she had to go to regain confident control of her
own life continued to overwhelm her emotionally. For weeks Sandy
wouldn't leave her sister Candy's apartment alone unless she were going to therapy. She wasn't afraid of breaking down and losing control
in front of the doctor or her sister, but other relationships felt
threatening.*

Living with Candy, Candy's husband, and their little girl proved a humbling adjustment for Sandy. She'd always prided herself on her independence. She'd always been the one who'd do the buying and the giving; suddenly being on the receiving end made her feel uneasy. At the same time, the unconditional love and acceptance shown by her sister flowed like a balm over a broken spirit that had felt so unlovable and unacceptable for so long.

Living in Atlanta again, for the first time in years, was disorienting. Everything had changed since Sandy had left it to begin flying nearly six years before. What she had expected to seem like being home again did little to aid in her search for the real Sandy Purl.

In October, Mike rented a U-Haul truck and brought to Atlanta all my stuff he'd taken from Denver to Florida. Just seeing Mike, when he walked into Candy's apartment, set my heart pounding. And the wrenching pain inside as I watched him drive away after he and my brother-in-law, Larry, unloaded the trailer reminded me how much I still loved him.

What Mike left behind pained me in another way. My clothes themselves nearly filled Candy and Larry's living room. Seven wardrobe boxes full of clothes! Many outfits still had the price tags on. And there were almost forty pairs of shoes.

Many of the outfits I'd received free when I'd done some modeling on days off in Atlanta. I was embarrassed by the size of the pile. Where and why had I ever accumulated such a horde of clothes? I'd worked in a uniform. On off days I'd always bummed around in blue jeans and Nik-Nik tops.

Standing there looking at these thousands of dollars worth of clothes and realizing I couldn't even get all the shoe boxes in the nearly empty closet of my bedroom, I also realized how much I'd changed. The obvious excesses of the old Sandy Purl shamed me.

I let Candy have her pick. I invited one of Candy's neighbors in to take what she liked. And I just gave much of the rest of it away.

In spite of all the adjustments I had to make in Atlanta, I felt my confidence and my strength increase nearly every day. With them grew my determination to press ahead until I had the control, the courage, and whatever else it took to begin work again as a flight attendant. The sooner the better.

I called Sandy Seagar, the Mohawk flight attendant whose name and number Del Mott had sent me; and through a series of long-distance calls we began to develop a meaningful and supportive relationship.

I needed all the support I could get in October when I went in to file my first deposition for all the legal actions resulting from the crash. I'd sued for damages to compensate for injuries, loss of wages, and emotional trauma. Mike had sued separately for the loss of his marriage. Of course, other survivors had also sued, as had the families of the dead crew and passengers.

I went downtown in Atlanta to a law office to give my sworn deposition in front of my own lawyer and those representing each of the defendants in the case (the manufacturers of the plane, the engines, and the radar, as well as the U.S. weather service, the Federal Aviation Administration, etc.). I surprised myself with my ability to hold up emotionally under the questioning of defense lawyers, who demanded to know, for example, "What authority did you have to begin briefing passengers for an emergency landing without instructions from the cockpit?"

For a long time, such an insinuation of irresponsibility on my part would have torn me up. But not now. I knew I'd done my job and done it well. While the questions angered me, and having to relive the memories still hurt, I had strength enough to survive the legal ordeal.

Perhaps the most difficult factor for me to accept was that the crash seemed to be ancient history for everyone else. They'd gone on with their lives. I was only now, after a year and a half, beginning to face what had happened with vision unblurred by drugs, alcohol, hysteria, or paranoia.

With the help God provided through Dr. Peek, Sandy Seagar, and my own family, especially Candy, the emotional flames and smoke began to clear and I gradually began to put the crash of Flight 242 in perspective. I finally realized that April 4, 1977, had been only one day in my life. But I'd let that one day dictate everything I'd felt, everything I'd done, every day since. I'd blamed everything wrong in my life, every bad day I had, on that crash. The awful truth was that everything that had happened since, I'd done to myself. I'd done far more harm to myself in Los Angeles with my summer-long drinking binge than the bruises and burns an airplane crash had inflicted.

These new insights didn't come without cost. How I regretted the wasted year and a half of futile running. I felt guilt for the hurt my reactions had caused so many others, such as my family and Mike.

I asked God to forgive it all. I believed He did, but the emotions only gradually loosened their grip.

As my perspective continued to clear about April 4, 1977, I also saw that my life had been only one of the many lives affected by the crash. I'd been so engulfed in my own reactions and inescapable memories that I'd never really considered or cared about what anyone else had suffered as a result of the crash. Not even my own sister.

Candy had told me her own story the summer after the crash. But it wasn't until now that I could understand and hurt for what she'd gone through.

The day before the crash, on one of my landings in Atlanta, I'd called her to say I was leaving several new spring and Easter outfits for my niece in the Southern Airways operations office at the airport. I'd always bought a lot of Aprill's clothes because I didn't have any daughters of my own and I had a little more money to spare than Candy did.

She'd asked if I was going to be back through Atlanta again that trip, and we agreed to meet the next afternoon during the brief layover before my last leg back to New Orleans. But I told her the weather predictions were bad and reminded her to call before she left home. She wrote down the number of the flight I'd be coming in on: Flight 242.

But on the afternoon of the fourth, Candy gave my mother a ride to the airport to pick up an old family friend who just happened to be coming to town. So she didn't bother to call ahead. She and my mother met the friend at the gate. When Candy stopped to get Aprill's clothes from the operations office and learned from a Southern employee that almost all flights were long delayed, she and my mother decided not to wait around for me.

A flash bulletin came over the car radio before they reached the expressway from the airport access road. The report stated only that Southern Airways Flight 242 had just crashed northwest of Atlanta and *that there were no survivors!*

My mother, sitting in the back seat, gasped and immediately began wailing, "Oh, God, no! My baby's dead, my baby's dead!"

As Candy told me this story, she said, "That's when I did the hardest thing I've ever done in my life. I whipped the car onto the shoulder and skidded to a halt. I turned around, looked Mama right in the face, and told her, 'Now you just hush up, Mama! You don't even know what flight Sandy was flying today!'

"Then I forced myself to pull back out on the highway and drove home knowing that in my pocketbook on the seat beside me was the piece of paper with a scribbled note that said, 'Sandy—#242.'

"Thank God, we no sooner got home than you called to say you were okay."

In the year and more that had passed since she first told me the story, I'd forgotten the details. So when Candy retold it that fall, we cried and held each other. Those first few weeks, we cried together a lot as I found the emotional strength to read through all the old clippings and follow-up stories about other people affected by the crash. Finally I was able to hurt and pray for other survivors and for the people of New Hope.

As the weeks passed and I felt better and stronger, I also felt a growing conviction that some of my biggest questions about my future, and about who I really was, weren't going to be answered until I actually walked back into that day in my past. I needed to return to the scene of the crash.

Chapter 13

Sandy made her plans to return to New Hope the second week of November. Candy arranged to be off work so she could go and offer her support. Ken Carollin, a newspaper columnist from New Jersey, who'd met Sandy at the awards ceremony in Washington back in June and had called periodically during the intervening months, asked if he could tag along. Sandy agreed.

My determination barely outweighed my anxiety as Candy and I walked into the terminal to meet Ken's flight. On the way back out to the car a few minutes later, I asked Ken if he'd like to stop somewhere for lunch. He said he'd just finished breakfast on the plane, but he didn't mind stopping if we wanted some.

"No, we just ate breakfast, too," Candy said. "I think we need to get on with it. We can get lunch later; it's only ten o'clock."

Ken squeezed into the back seat of my Opel, and Candy climbed in on the passenger's side. "You sure you know the way?" she asked me, as I accelerated down the entry ramp to merge into the expressway traffic.

"Of course," I said impatiently.

But the miles sped by as we headed west on I-20 out of Atlanta. I began filling Ken in on my recent progress in therapy, and I still didn't have him up to date when Candy spotted the "Welcome to Alabama" sign. We'd gone too far.

So we turned around and headed east again. I concluded my original monologue and went right on to talk about New Hope and list the things I wanted to be sure and see. I didn't stop talking until Candy blurted out, "Sandy! That was the exit. You missed it again."

I chuckled nervously and quipped, "Maybe you can't get there by road. Maybe you have to drop out of the sky." No one else laughed.

We exited at the next possible turnoff, and I headed cross-country on back roads. But after a few intersections where we could only guess which way to turn, Candy insisted we pull into a gas station and ask the way to New Hope.

A few minutes after getting directions we were on Georgia Route 92 and fast approaching New Hope. Just ahead I spotted a sign saying, "Martin's Ambulance Service." I felt my insides tighten as I pointed and told Candy and Ken, "They were the first ambulances to reach the scene of the crash."

I knew we were close. There were no more exits to miss. New Hope lay just ahead. And as I pulled to a stop at the intersection where Highway 92 forms a "T" with Spur 92, I had to grip the steering wheel with all my strength to stop my hands from shaking.

"This is it," I said quietly.

This was the spot where the plane had first touched down. Across the road was the fire station. Just to the right stood the Amoco station. I took a long, deep breath before I whispered, "Okay, let's go" and turned down Spur 92, following the same path the plane had taken.

"Right there is where the wing must have clipped the utility pole. And that building on the left must be Newman's Store. It's been rebuilt." I drove slowly down the road, talking and pointing. But when we reached the last house on the edge of town, I still hadn't seen the crash site itself, the trees where most of the plane's pieces had finally come to rest.

"We passed it, Sandy. It's back there," Ken said.

"No, it couldn't be. There were trees all around out close to the road." But Ken convinced me to pull over, and he showed me a map. We turned around and went back.

"Right there," Ken said.

"No, there were trees when I came out of the plane, and there was a driveway, and I went to a house . . . that house . . . no, I don't know." I nearly cried in confusion. I'd been here only once in my life, but a thousand times in my dreams. And nothing looked familiar.

"Let's go back to Newman's Store," suggested Candy. "Maybe someone there can help us."

With my heart racing, I pulled up to the brick grocery with the Union 76 pumps in the front. We piled out of the car, and I entered the little country store first.

When my eyes adjusted to the dim indoor light, I saw four men sitting in chairs along one wall. Walking toward them, I asked, "Would one of you gentlemen happen to be Mr. Newman?"

A short heavyset man with white hair and wearing bib overalls stood up and held out his hand. "I'm Charlie Newman," he said. "And you're Sandy Purl. I'd recognize you anywhere."

Sandy and Mr. Newman embraced like family. Though they'd never met, they both seemed to feel a common bond. Both had seen their lives radically changed by a single event. The Newmans' store had been completely destroyed in the fire resulting from the exploding gas tanks in front of the store. Insurance had rebuilt the store, but the Newmans had never owned the building; they leased it. They lost a lot of business during the months of rebuilding, the total of which had to be disputed with Southern's insurance carriers. The family members they lost could never be replaced. The three mothers and five children who'd been parked in front of the store when the plane smashed through their car were all Mrs. Newman's nieces and great-nephews and -nieces. Sandy had known this from the newspaper accounts.

After Mr. Newman and I talked for a couple of minutes, he said, "Well, you just stay put a minute, I need to go call the missus and tell her you've come."

"How is Mrs. Newman?" I asked.

He stopped and turned toward me, looking a little sad. "Not so good. She cries a lot. And she never wants to work here at the store anymore. It brings it all back."

"Then maybe we shouldn't ask her to come down. You can just tell—"

"Oh, no," he chuckled. "She'd have me shot if she knew you'd been here and I hadn't called her!" He walked over and reached down under the cash register and pulled out an old rotary phone. Setting it up on the counter, he dialed his wife. "Come on down to the store," he told her. "Sandy, the stewardess, has come back."

No sooner had Mr. Newman put the receiver down than I heard

a siren. Faintly, off in the distance at first. I covered my face with my hands. "Oh, no, please God, no." My knees buckled, but Candy caught me. Her arms held me tight as an ambulance from Martin's Ambulance Service raced by the store with lights flashing and siren screaming.

As the sound receded down the road, in the same direction so many wailing ambulances had gone on that afternoon nineteen months before, I shook. I sobbed on Candy's shoulder. Everyone in the store stood watching, knowing. I told myself, "I'm going to be strong. Not just for myself, but for them." A few seconds later, I rubbed the last of the tears from my eyes and said, loud enough to reassure everyone in the little store, "I'm sorry. I'm okay now. Everything's okay."

I introduced myself to everyone who came into the store. One middle-aged, portly woman, with a lovely smile and sparkling eyes, shook my hand over and over again. She introduced herself as Mrs. Robert Craton; she explained that her elderly mother-in-law, Berlie Maye Craton, had been struck and killed by the plane as she'd been walking out by the road. When I told her I was confused about where the crash had actually ended up, Mrs. Craton tugged me out of the store to give me a walking tour.

"Honey, you're just confused because those big pine trees are gone now. They all burned—flared up with all that pitch, you know—and had to be cut down," Mrs. Craton said as we traipsed along the road. Then she stopped and pointed at some tall milkweeds and wild grasses. "Right over there I found my mother-in-law's body. I pulled her back into that yard, away from the fire. Later, when I saw all the rescue people hauling bodies up to that bus, I dragged her off behind that house and hid her body so we wouldn't lose her among all the others." I stopped and looked at her for a moment in shock, as she gestured across the yards.

When she finished her account, she walked a little way and stopped once more. "That's where your part of the plane was," she pointed. "The other girl's section ended up over there. And way down there by that house was the pilots' cabin. Flames were shooting higher than the tallest trees. Bodies lay everywhere, all over the ground. I even saw some on roofs and up in the branches."

As she talked and pointed, I began to see where I was. "Now I remember!" I exclaimed. "There's the driveway I ran out on, I didn't see it before. I must have dragged the bodies over there. There's the little house where I ran to try to use the phone. And later I must have run to that house over there to use the bathroom. Can you believe that? In the middle of all that, I had to take a pee.

"And that means—" I stopped and turned to survey the area again. In my mind I could picture the scene from the nightmares, the one of the man in a light-blue suit. His seat had broken free of the wreckage and finally come to a stop midway between the biggest piece of the plane and one of the engines. I'd seen him there that day and countless times since in my dreams, his arms reaching out, struggling to get free from his seatbelt. The next instant, I also saw in my mind an empty seat. All the guilt came flooding back and I remembered searching the emergency room, looking for someone in a blue suit.

"There was a man, trapped in his seat, over there," I pointed for Mrs. Craton. "I never saw what happened to him."

"I remember," she said. "He was one of the few I saw alive. Two men lifted him out of the seat and took him to an ambulance. It looked like he'd be okay."

At Mrs. Craton's words, something happened in the depths of my soul. A gigantic anchor of guilt had been cut loose.

For the next twenty minutes, I talked out my own memories. "There's where the ambulances lined up. The bus was parked there, the bodies stacked here." At every turn I recalled images I hadn't ever consciously remembered. I saw faces that had never appeared in any of the nightmares. I relived the whole thing once more.

Seeing New Hope again, hearing how others had been affected, walking through the crash site, and replaying the terrible tragedy through my mind all triggered an immense sadness inside. Yet something about this emotional reaction was different from any emotion I'd felt before.

In spite of the growing pain I felt for Mrs. Craton, the Newmans, and the rest of the town of New Hope, the longer I walked and talked along that highway, the stronger I felt. I sensed the awful burden of the memories loosening their grip on my life. By the time we started back for the store, I felt nearly buoyant.

Before Mrs. Craton left for her home, I hugged her and thanked her for walking with me. I asked if there was anything I should do, or anything I shouldn't say when I met Mrs. Newman. "Just do what I do," Mrs. Craton advised. "Just hold her and cry with her when she cries."

When I walked back into the store, I immediately spotted a stocky woman standing by the counter with Mr. Newman. As she turned to me at the sound of the door, I could see tiredness in her sad face and in the blue eyes magnified by large-frame glasses. "I'm Mildred Newman," she said, walking toward me. We embraced and I heard her sobbing over and over, "My Sandy, my Sandy." In the hour that followed, the Newmans and I shared our own stories of April 4, 1977.

"All those girls and their babies who were killed in that car were relatives of mine," Mrs. Newman began, tears already filling her eyes. "They were waiting for me to go with 'em. I'd gone out with them, but I'd forgotten something. To this day I don't remember what it was. So I walked back in the store for whatever it was, and a customer asked me to ring up a bunch of bananas, because Charlie was busy on the other side of the store. Can you believe my life was saved by a bunch of bananas?"

She went on to explain that while she was making change for the customer, the plane struck the gas pumps outside. "I thought it was a tornado," she said. "We'd heard one was in the area."

"The next second the pumps exploded and the flames came bursting through the windows. I don't remember what I did after that. I know I screamed. For some reason God must have put his shield around me, while those young folks in the car were all killed."

Mildred Newman broke into sobs and couldn't continue. Following Mrs. Craton's advice, I put my arms around her and let her cry. To my own astonishment, I didn't cry with her. I just didn't feel the need. For the first time in nineteen months, I found the strength to hurt without emotionally falling apart.

Charlie Newman took up the story where Mrs. Newman left off. "Mildred ran into the bathroom to hide. Me and the customers had to drag her out. We barely made it out through the back door before the roof caved."

Through her tears, Mrs. Newman continued. "Our daughter and little granddaughter had been parked out front alongside the other car. I was sure they were dead, too."

Mr. Newman started in again. "We hadn't seen our daughter pull away just seconds before the crash. She told us later she was at the intersection just up the road when the plane just missed the top of her car. She looked back to see the explosion and thought we were all killed.

"Our younger daughter also thought we'd been killed. In the confusion afterward, we couldn't find each other. The younger girl spent half the night looking through burned bodies in the morgue trying to find us."

The Newmans volunteered some additional information about their own hassles with the airline and the insurance. And Sandy recounted a lot of things that had happened to her. She was surprised at how much the Newmans already knew, until Mrs. Newman explained that she'd read every clipping she could find on the crash and its survivors. She'd been following Sandy's story whenever it made the news.

Word spread quickly through New Hope; many people dropped in to meet Sandy. She listened sympathetically to those who wanted to share their own experiences on that April afternoon. When those memories brought them to tears, Sandy would reach out and hold a hand or touch an arm to try to comfort them. But she didn't cry.

Mrs. Craton left for a while, but she came back to the store to talk with me again. "It's my husband," she explained. "He's been sick or he'd have come over himself to meet you. But he asked me to come back and ask if you saw his mother that day.

"He hasn't slept well since the crash; he keeps thinking his mother suffered something terrible. Did you see her at all? Can I tell him she didn't suffer?"

I tried to remember, but I couldn't. "There were so many, I may have seen her," I said. "I really don't know. But if she was hit by the plane, she must have died instantly. She wouldn't have suffered. Tell your husband he can rest easier about that."

Mrs. Craton wrote down everything I'd said. Then she kissed me and hurried off to report every word to her husband.

Candy, Ken, and I were getting ready to leave when Mrs. Newman ducked behind the store's counter and pulled out an old tin box. Reaching in, she drew out a folded collage of taped-together paper, torn pieces of writing paper, business cards, even credit card receipts. On each scrap was scribbled a name and an address. This haphazard list was Mrs. Newman's record of the survivors of Flight 242—survivors who'd felt compelled to come back to New Hope.

"You see," said Mrs. Newman, "you're not the first. A lot of the others have already been here. But I knew you'd come back, Sandy. I knew you'd make it, because I've been praying for you."

I had to kiss her for that. And as I bid my goodbyes and heard all the "Y'all come back now's," I promised I would indeed come back.

Candy and Ken figured Sandy would be wiped out by her emotional afternoon. When she surprised them by proposing a trip to Paulding Memorial Hospital, they asked if she was sure she wanted to go. She replied that she really wanted to see the doctors, nurses, and other staff people who had been so kind to her.

So, without a moment's uncertainty about the route she'd only been over once, and that in the back of speeding highway patrol car, Sandy drove right from New Hope to Paulding Memorial Hospital in Dallas, Georgia. Ken tried to warn her that a reception from the medical staff of a hospital emergency ward probably wouldn't be as cordial as the response she'd found in New Hope. That didn't deter Sandy. She marched in through the emergency room doors and with her two companions in tow, she headed straight for the receptionist's desk.

"Hi," she announced. "My name is Sandy. I was one of the steward-esses in the New Hope plane crash last year, and I've come back to meet the people who took care of me."

For a long moment the woman just stared at Sandy without saying a word. Then she ushered the three visitors into a nearby office and be-gan making a series of quick phone calls. Within moments, the proces-sion began to arrive—doctors, nurses, x-ray technicians, orderlies, and hospital administrators.

For the next couple of hours, they recounted every cut and burn Sandy had. They shook their heads about how they'd almost had to strap her in bed to keep her from visiting her passengers. And they laughed with her about the decoy ambulance plan they used to get Sandy past the press waiting outside the hospital. They took Sandy on a quickie tour of the whole hospital, pointing out her room, Cathy's room, and the rooms of other survivors who'd stayed in the hospital overnight. Sandy wept silently for a minute or two when they showed her the plaque on the door of Room 310. It read, "Dedicated in loving memory of Captain William McKenzie and First Officer Lyman Keele by Southern Airways Employees."

When the tour ended, Sandy went with a number of the staff to the cafeteria for coffee. There, one of the hospital officials asked if Sandy would be willing to come back sometime to take part in an actual dedi-cation of the room honoring the pilots; Sandy said she'd be happy to. She told everyone who could stay about her emotional struggles and the long, winding pilgrimage that had finally brought her back. Thus an afternoon that could have ended as just one more emotionally trau-matic episode in Sandy's life in fact more closely resembled the re-union of a group of lifelong friends.

There's no way to adequately describe my feelings as I pulled the car out of that hospital parking lot and headed for home. The day had been so full. My mind was spinning with new memories. Even when I'd been running across the country to get away from it all, I think I always knew I would have to come back. Now I had.

In one sense, the events of April 4, 1977, had never seemed so real as they had when I walked along the site of that crash again. The return to New Hope gave me a perspective nothing else had brought. It shamed me to realize how many people's lives had been torn apart by the crash, and in contrast, how little damage had been done to me, yet how poorly I'd reacted. I felt truly humbled when I realized that Mrs. Newman, who'd lost so much herself, had been praying for me.

For me, the trip back to New Hope was like cleaning and closing a raw, infected wound that had lain open for months. Seeing the site again, with the wreckage cleared and green grass growing again on the once-charred earth, helped me believe it when I told myself, "It's over. It's really over."

Chapter 14

For a year and a half, the name of the town where we crashed had seemed a cruel irony. My career, my marriage, life as I'd known it, had all come to what seemed like a hopeless end because of what had happened there. Only now, after my second visit to the little country crossroads, did the name New Hope seem to fit.

As I drove back to Atlanta, and reran the memory tape again and again in my mind over the next few days, it seemed to me, from the reactions of everyone I'd met, that I'd been able to encourage them as much as they had helped me. That gave me a deep, satisfied sense of usefulness I hadn't known for a long time. It also gave me the first glimmer of hope that I'd be able to find some way, any way, to use my experience to help others.

This hope, fueled by my continuing therapy, gave rise to enough new courage and determination for me to make another major step. Dr. Peek made the arrangements with Southern for me to regain my pass-riding privileges, and I made plans for my first Southern Airways flight since 242.

My brother-in-law drove me to the airport on the afternoon of November 18. When we approached the terminal and he pulled into the lane marked "Short-term Parking," I asked him just to drop me at the departure doors.

"I'll be glad to walk in with you," he said.

"No," I insisted. "I want to do this by myself." I knew Larry meant well and just wanted to be supportive. But I didn't want anyone watching or worrying over me. For me, this was a very personal event, another important milestone in my recovery. So I would walk to my flight by myself, just as I'd done a thousand times before. I wanted everything to be as low-key as possible. So it was, until I got to the ticket counter.

I knew the ticket agent. She greeted me warmly and asked how I was doing. As we chatted over the counter, I felt a tap on my shoulder and turned around to encounter a vaguely familiar young man in his early thirties. Before I could place him, he introduced himself. "I'm Scott Newell," he said. "Channel 11 News." Then I noticed a cameraman standing behind him and a young woman, who introduced herself as a reporter for the *Atlanta Constitution*.

For a few moments, I just stood there, feeling invaded. "Where did they come from?" I thought. "How did they know I would be here? I didn't say anything."

"Sandy," the ticket agent motioned me toward the counter. "You can come through here and go to the gate through the restricted area if you want," she whispered. "You don't have to talk to them."

Her offer tempted me. All I'd wanted was a routine flight, and here was the press wanting to make it a media event. Then I thought of all the other times my story had made front-page news, I thought of Mrs. Newman and who knows how many other people who'd followed those accounts and prayed for me. So I decided to make the best of a bad situation to at least fill in the blanks of my experience. Perhaps I could use this time to make a declaration of progress.

Very slowly I turned back around toward the camera and the questioners to ask, "What is it you want?"

The TV reporter told me he knew I had come to take my first Southern flight since the crash. He wanted to talk to me about my feelings and go with me to the gate. I surrendered without a fight. "Okay," I said.

"Where are you going on your flight today?"

"First I'm going to Washington, and then I'm flying on to Philadelphia before returning to Atlanta. It's just a short trip to visit a couple of friends." (I didn't tell them I was going to Washington to visit Sandy Seagar, the flight attendant who'd survived the Mohawk crash.)

"Is this your very first flight since the crash?"

"No, I've made several flights with different carriers. This is just my first flight with Southern."

"How has your experience changed your life?"

What could I say? I had a flight leaving in just a few minutes. I said, "I think from now on, I'll eat more ice cream and pick more flowers."

Even as we headed for the gate, the two reporters plied me with more questions while the cameraman hurried ahead to shoot us walking into the camera and dropped behind to capture our image walking away. When we reached the gate, we stopped and talked some more.

"Are you afraid as you approach this flight?" he asked.

He probably had noticed my shaking hands. "No," I replied honestly. "But I am anxious. My hands shake. My body still reacts to what I've been through. But I've been able to accept the fact that's normal for me. I may shake every time I get on a plane for the rest of my life. But I know that with God's help I can handle it."

With that, I turned and went through the gate door and walked out across the asphalt rampway. At the top of the airplane steps, I looked back toward the terminal windows to see the faces of the reporters alongside the TV camera recording my departure. I waved once for the camera and ducked into the plane—a DC-9.

Sandy never saw the report that Mrs. Newman and who knows how many other people witnessed that night on the evening news. The clip first included some of Sandy's comments about her encouraging progress. Then the footage showing her walking slowly out to the plane was interrupted with file film of the crash scene. As she started up the steps, the report cut to pictures of rescue workers carrying bodies out of the wreckage. As she reached the top of the steps, the scene faded to smoldering pieces of airplane littering the ground. Then finally, there was Sandy, waving at the camera and ducking into the airplane. But by the time that newsclip aired, Sandy had reached the first destination on her trip—Washington, D.C.

After the emotional test of the media gauntlet at the airport, the flight itself seemed almost anticlimactic. It was made easier by the fact that the B-flight attendant was a good friend who hugged me and let me know that she was ready to help any way she could to make the flight easier for me.

I met Sandy Seagar in the Washington Dulles terminal and went home with her for the evening. Our friendship, which had begun to bud during the phone conversations we'd had over the preceding few weeks, now blossomed in our first face-to-face encounter. We talked about her feelings and mine about the memories of the crashes. We shared our anger and our guilt. We talked about the reactions of other people to us and many other feelings and experiences we'd shared.

It was the scrapbooks that really cemented our bond. She looked at mine with the newspaper headlines and the photos of the crash. Then I thumbed through hers. When I came to the photo, the chills ran from my head to my heels. "How awful!" I thought as I studied the newspaper picture of the tail of an airplane protruding from the home into which it had crashed. A thick blanket of snow surrounded the flame-scorched home, in which residents had died. As I tried to imagine how this other Sandy had escaped from that wreckage, the realization hit me: "Here is one of only a handful of people on earth who is capable of understanding what I've been through. And she *does* understand."

When I flew out of Washington the next day, I had a new friend who not only could understand anything I wanted to say about my experience, she also understood those things I *couldn't* say. I belonged to a very small group of people—airplane crash survivors. But another living, breathing human being had been where I'd been. I wasn't alone.

An even more reassuring event occurred within days after my visit in Washington with Sandy.

One sunny day early in December, I went for an afternoon visit to my grandmother's in Atlanta. As I talked with her, she pulled out a box of old family photos and memorabilia I'd been through countless times in the past. I took the box and sat on her living-room floor to sift through the contents as we continued our visit.

There were fuzzy family snapshots, ancient-looking prints of my grandparents, photos of my own parents when they were young. And a couple of yellowed newspaper articles I'd never stopped to notice before.

"What are these?"I asked, holding up the clippings.

"Those are about your father when he was in the service," my grandmother explained as I began to read.

The first and longer article gave an account of a fire aboard a Swedish transport vessel docked near Kindley Air Force Base in Bermuda, where my father was stationed. His Air Force firefighting crew got a call to help battle the fire below deck on this ship. The fire chief, one of the ship's officers, and my father had donned gas masks and gone down in the hold to try to pinpoint the source of the blaze. When the other two men collapsed from the fumes, my father dragged the body of his chief to safety and went back down for the officer. He'd gotten the officer almost out of the hold when the man's belt caught in a doorway, and as he tried to free the man, he felt the initial effects of the fumes and retreated quickly to the deck, where he passed out. Other firefighters reentered the hold to search for the officer but couldn't find him. When my father came to a few minutes later, his colleagues had to physically restrain him from going back into the hold. The newspaper said he shouted at the men holding him back, "Let me go get him! Let me *go*, dammit! I know where to look for him!"

The man died before other firefighters found him and dragged him to the deck. What struck me about the clipping were two similarities to my own experience. My father had been overcome by deadly fumes, and once he had escaped he fought, in an attempt to carry out his duty, with those who tried to help him. Even his words reminded me of my own reaction at the crash site, when I had shouted, "Let me go! I have to find the cockpit. I can identify parts of the plane no one else will know."

But it was the second article about a different incident that shook me to my soul. The dateline also read, "Kindley AFB, Bermuda." The date on the clipping said, "February 1, 1950," and the headline read, "Two Airmen Decorated at Parade and Review." I

scanned the article until I reached the part about my father's deco-
ration for an incident that had happened a couple years before.

The article said,

The Soldier's Medal was awarded to S/Sgt. Thomas Purl of the 1604th
Air Installations Squadron for an act of heroism that found him entering
the flaming wreckage of a burning aircraft to extricate the pilot who was
trapped in the flames. Despite lack of protective clothing and with complete disregard for the imminent danger of an explosion, Sgt. Purl
climbed aboard the burning craft and successfully extricated the trapped
pilot. For these actions, beyond the call of duty, which took place at the
Marietta, Georgia Air Base, Sgt. Purl was decorated.

My hands trembled so violently I could hardly see the letters on
the page as I read again the words, "Marietta, Georgia Air Base."
That was now called Dobbins' Air Force base, the airfield we were
trying to reach when Flight 242 went down. Thirty years before
the day I'd seen my father's image in the smoke and flames of a
crashed DC-9, he'd gone into another burning aircraft just a few
miles from New Hope, Georgia. And just as surely as that old clipping proved his heroism back in the 1940s, it proved for me his
presence on April 4, 1977.

The emotion of that moment prompted a hasty goodbye to my
grandmother. I couldn't explain my reaction to her because I'd
sheltered her from all talk about the crash. But on the drive home I
felt I'd fairly burst with exhilaration. After so many long months
of tormenting silence, after all the doubts about my own sanity,
that clipping said to me, *"He was there. I did see him. He was there!"*

Before I got back to Candy's, something that had been a deeply
buried memory clicked into my conscious mind: "The book! The
one that woman gave me at the hearings. What was its name?
What was it about? What does that book have to do with this afternoon? With Daddy?" I didn't know the reason for my sudden rec-
ollection of that book, but I thought I knew right where to find it.

The moment I walked through the apartment door, I headed
right for my bedroom. I spotted the box in the top of the closet and
pulled it down. The first thing I saw when I opened it was my uniform. Under that I uncovered the transcripts of the NTSB hear-

ings, my serving apron, and several other work-related items I'd had no need for and wanted no part of since the crash. Underneath it all was the book.

I lifted it from the box and read the title, *Life After Life*, by Raymond Moody. I scanned the dustjacket, then opened the book.

Soon I was shaking again with the same intense emotions I'd felt an hour before as I'd read those clippings. This book reported account after account from people on the verge of death who had experienced out-of-body sensations very much like what had happened to me in the plane crash. They talked of leaving their bodies, hovering above the scene, looking down at themselves, an incredible feeling of peace, a reluctance to return to their bodies, and in some cases even encounters with someone they knew who had preceded them into death. Nearly every case I read about shared something in common with my own experience.

I didn't read the entire book that afternoon. I couldn't. I had to quit when my tears of joy blurred my vision. I closed the book and I whispered to myself over and over and over again, "I'm not crazy. I'm really not crazy!"

That assurance was intoxicating, liberating. First the clippings, now the book. I knew without doubt that the one memory of the crash that had tormented me more than any of the nightmares would trouble me no more. The combined circumstances of this afternoon convinced me that what I'd been allowed to experience wasn't something I should ever try to forget. Instead, it had been a privileged spiritual encounter. It wasn't something I should hide for fear of being judged, it was something I could, even *should* talk about.

The next morning I came out of my room to find Candy sitting alone at the kitchen table nursing a cup of coffee. "I learned something important yesterday about my mental health," I said. And I told her about seeing Daddy, about my fears of insanity, the clippings, and the book. I cried with relief as I talked, and Candy cried with me. When I finished she said, "Oh, Sandy, I'm so sorry. I never knew how much you were carrying inside."

But it was hidden inside no longer.

Once Sandy told her story, her whole story, it seemed very much a story that needed to be told. Not only Sandy felt that way; people who heard about her experience also felt it. In December, at a Sunday evening service at her home church, Sandy listened to a guest speaker talk about the work of an organization called Greater Atlanta Youth for Christ, a nationally affiliated group working with high school students. After the service, Sandy introduced herself to the speaker, who directed the Atlanta YFC program, and arranged an appointment to learn more. A few weeks later when they met for lunch, Sandy shared her own story. Like most Atlantans, the man remembered the crash and publicity about the survivors. He was so moved by Sandy's story he asked her if she'd be willing to share the story of her emotional and spiritual pilgrimage at an upcoming conference of young people from around Atlanta. She agreed, and put it on her calendar for early in March.

But even before her first speaking opportunity, Sandy met and told her story to one of the editors of Campus Life *magazine, a nationally distributed Christian publication for high school and college-age readers. This editor was impressed with the potential her story had for inspiring others; he asked if he could come to Atlanta to interview her again a few months later, and he began making plans to give Sandy's story a major treatment in* Campus Life.

In the months following that first Southern Airways flight, I used my flying privileges quite a number of times. The company wouldn't provide me with an official Southern identity card, so getting passes for each flight proved to be an emotional hassle. I had to show a memo each time I wanted a pass and explain why I didn't have an ID card, who I was, etc., etc. Inevitably, the person who looked at the memo then had to say something or ask something about the crash. But eventually I got used to it; and I wanted to fly enough to go through the annoying procedure.

I didn't have much money, so when I flew I mostly visited friends. Each trip got a little easier, the physical reactions a little less. The flights helped recondition me for my ongoing goal of going back to work. They also enabled me to return to the places I'd been and to see the people I'd encountered since the crash. I took the opportunity to apologize to some of these people and explain to them what I'd been going through—that I'd been a monster in my own eyes. And that I'd changed.

But apparently the difference was obvious. My Denver friends especially noticed the change. "You're just not the same person, Sandy," they told me. "You're so much more alive. You even laugh."

Through the eyes of those friends who'd seen me at my worst, I was able to see how far I'd come. In the time with Dr. Peek, we had concentrated much of our efforts on my self-image. I'd hated what I had become for so long that I needed help in spotting good aspects of myself, talents, and strengths. Now I began to like what I saw.

Of course, my family greatly bolstered my self-worth as well. I realized I'd spent my whole life trying to win the approval of my parents and family. When I left home and began to work, I often used my money to give them things and do things for them; and while I did so partly out of love, I also did so partly to win their acceptance and gratitude. But now I had no job, and couldn't pay for anything. And they loved me anyway! What a wonderful realization!

My new spiritual awareness helped, too. Some people describe their crisis spiritual experiences as being "born again." But for me, turning to God in that Salt Lake City mental ward had been more like being given my self, my real self. In so many of the experiences that followed, especially the "firsts"—my first visit with Dr. Peek, my first trip back to New Hope, the first Southern flight, etc.—I had discovered a little more of that self. Some of what I discovered seemed to be lost remnants of the old, precrash Sandy. Some felt entirely new. I sensed my life changing.

And all the change felt somehow purposeful and controlled. After wandering and running for so long, I can't describe how wonderful it was to feel guided.

On March 10, 1979, Sandy Purl tried to describe how God had led her through and after the plane crash when she told her story as scheduled to the Youth for Christ conference. This too turned out to be

another first—the first time Sandy had publicly described her experi-
ence since she testified at the NTSB hearings two months after the
crash. A number of young people responded to her story by making
their own spiritual commitments to God.

Someone who had heard me speak at the youth retreat got me
an invitation to tell my story at a local church. Again I cried my
way through. But I could sense the congregation's response. I
knew God had used me and my experience once again to speak to
people.

Those two experiences of sharing my story in public gave me
renewed courage to follow through on my promise to go back to
New Hope and Paulding Memorial Hospital once again. Scott
Newell of Channel 11 again accompanied me, as part of his coverage of the second anniversary of the crash. On April 3, 1979, I
again walked through the crash site, visited the Newmans, and
took part in the official dedication service of the plaque in Paulding Memorial Hospital memorializing Captain William McKenzie
and First Officer Lyman Keele. There in the hospital so full of
memories from that horrible night two years before, I read aloud
the verses from Psalm 122: "May they prosper who love you.
Peace be within your walls, and security within your towers. For
my brethren and companions' sake, I will say, 'Peace be within
you.'

Channel 11 carried clips of Sandy reading at the dedication service
along with an interview. A second TV station included an interview
with her, as did several radio stations doing two-year anniversary re-
ports on April 4. In one interview, Sandy explained, "I'm hurting, I'm
sad, I'm mourning." But those who had followed her story for two
years saw new hope in her words when she told the Atlanta public,
"At this point in my life I'm putting my puzzle back together. I'm not
sure where I am or where I'm going. But I am determined to go for-
ward and use this experience as a way of showing people that I'm an
answer to a lot of prayers prayed two years ago. I'm proof that God
answers prayer."

Sandy told the media about her own prayer between those two bath-
rooms of the burning DC-9. She'd felt something lift her up, the flames

parted, and she stepped out on solid ground. She thanked the public for their prayers for the victims of the crash on that day and since. Sandy admitted she would like to be a flight attendant again some day. She also admitted her doubts and acknowledged the fact she had a long way to go before returning to work.

In everything she said rang a strong, clear note of optimism. One of the announcers on a series of WSB radio reports echoed her feelings: "Today Sandy Purl knows why God allowed her to live through that plane crash . . . And with the help of God, she's beginning to live again."

Chapter 15

On Wednesday, April 4, 1979, the two-year anniversary of the crash, I picked up the afternoon edition of the *Atlanta Journal* to find my picture at the top of page one. The headline running across the entire front page proclaimed, "Crash Site Beckons Stewardess."

The article recounted the dedication ceremony at Paulding the day before, talked of the "fraternity" between me and the people of New Hope, quoted some of what I'd told the reporter about my first visit to New Hope back in November, and summarized in a few paragraphs a little of what had happened to me since the crash—my wandering, divorce, pay cutoff, and continuing psychological trauma. I smiled with satisfaction when I finished reading the article, because it spoke about my "religious awakening" and acknowledged my new perspective and my understanding of how small I was in the face of such a devastating tragedy.

This was the message I wanted people to see. I wanted to let everyone know that God had brought me through my whole experience. I also wanted the public to recognize the bigger picture, to feel compassion for all the other survivors, for the people of New Hope, for those who died and their families. And I felt very pleased by the "memorial" tone of all the second anniversary news coverage; it gave me a chance to grieve in a way I'd been too numbed to do two years before. It also drained me so much emotionally that I felt as if I'd just been through the death and funeral of a dear friend. When all the reports had been aired or printed, all I wanted was a chance for rest, quiet, and reflection.

But Sandy didn't get rest. One television news report had included on-camera quotes from Candy as well as from Sandy. And during Candy's comments they'd flashed her name and hometown on the screen. And since her town was small and her last name uncommon, anyone watching could go to the Atlanta phone book and in sixty seconds find the phone number of the apartment where the twin sisters lived.

Instead of peace and quiet in the wake of her most recent public exposure, Sandy began receiving a string of phone calls. Some came from friends who'd lost touch and just wished to say hello. Many others came from total strangers who called to say they remembered her story and wished her the best. But not all were so kind.

Talking to the press about the anniversary had proved an emotional strain, but one I'd wanted to endure. In fact, I'd been thrilled with my own composure and endurance. Seeing and hearing the reports in the media had doubled the strain, but again, I'd held up. The phone calls, however, literally sucked what little emotional strength I had left right out of me.

Middle of the morning, April 7, I heard the phone ring again. I walked into the kitchen and picked it up.

"Hello."

"Is this Sandy Purl?"

"Yes it is."

"I just want you to know," a harsh female voice said. "My baby died in that crash, and I won't rest until everyone else does."

I gave out a sharp cry as I let the receiver drop from my hand and clatter on the floor. A few seconds passed before I picked it up and placed it back on its cradle. Then I just stood there, holding my head, and moaned, "I don't believe this. Why are they doing this to me? What did I do?"

For the rest of that day, I refused to answer the phone. And when friends of Candy's dropped by the apartment that evening, I quickly retreated to my bedroom to be alone until they were gone.

I prayed a lot that week. I demanded answers from God to a lot of questions: "Am I ever going to be able to put the crash experience behind me? Why am I still so tormented? Is this a sign that I'm supposed to quit thinking and talking about my experience and go on with life? Is it time to let go and quit hurting others by talking about my own experience? How long is therapy going to take before I can be free from the terrible emotional aftermath of that crash? It's been two years; is life ever going to be normal again?"

I prayed and I cried and I prayed some more. But I heard no answer. "I want some answer," I said to God. "I need—no, I *deserve* some answers."

Still I heard nothing.

That Friday, a friend called. It had been a while since we'd talked, but I knew she was into parapsychology. She'd heard me comment on the radio that I still didn't know exactly where I was going or what lay ahead for me, and she called to suggest a way I could find out.

"There's a psychic fair this weekend," she said. "At the Foundation of Truth in Atlanta." She went on to say she'd been taking a couple of courses from one of the psychics who would be there, and she thought what I really needed was some life readings. We chatted a while, I told her I'd think about her advice, and we said goodbye.

The next morning I called Steve, a friend I'd gone out with a few times, with whom I'd planned a picnic later that day out at Stone Mountain. I asked if he'd mind leaving earlier and going with me to the Foundation of Truth, and he said fine.

We parked my car on the street and walked a couple of blocks through the fresh spring air. The Foundation of Truth was located in a beautiful old southern mansion, an antebellum structure complete with columns on the front. A small crowd of people milled about the porch, talking, waiting for something. The moment Steve and I walked through the door and into a front foyer, I thought to myself, "Sandy, you don't belong here." I had never felt more out of place in my life, and I felt sure that everyone in the place was noticing my uneasiness. "Come on," I told myself, "you're just a nameless face in the crowd." I felt as visible as an intruder carrying a flickering candle into a pitch-black room.

"But you're here, you may as well go through with it," I urged myself. So I signed in at the registration table and took a number to wait for a reading from the same psychic my friend had studied under. Then Steve and I wandered back out to the fresh air and the sunshine on the porch to wait. Outdoors, some of the oppressive atmosphere I'd felt lifted. Yet with each passing minute I felt more and more uneasy. And my number wasn't much closer to being called than when we walked in.

"This is crazy," I told Steve after about twenty minutes. "We'll be here all day. Let's go back and see whom else I could talk to." At the registration table, I read through the list of psychics until I came to a man's name with the title "Rev." in front of it. I noticed he was from Florida. "Perfect," I said to myself. "He won't know me from all the news coverage around Atlanta." When I saw he was booked up all day, I took a Monday afternoon appointment and said to Steve, "Let's get out of here. I'll come back by myself after the weekend when there isn't such a crowd."

But as we worked our way back out the door and across the porch toward the street through the milling crowd, I noticed a man watching me. Balding, with wire-rimmed glasses, wearing casual slacks and shirt, he looked like a middle-aged accountant on his day off. He walked toward us and stood blocking our way down the steps.

"Can I talk to you for a few moments?" he asked me. Before I could brush him off, he began talking again. His eyes began to glaze over, but they were penetrating nevertheless. Shivers tip-toed up my spine as I heard him say, "You have just gotten over an infection. You're doing wonderfully physically. But something has been bothering you . . ." He was obviously a psychic. So far everything he was saying about me seemed uncannily accurate.

With difficulty, I forced my eyes away from his and down to the name tag on his shirt. He paused, and I exclaimed, "Why, I've got a life reading scheduled with you Monday afternoon!"

The glaze faded, and his eyes focused on mine again. "Oh, good," he said. "No need to talk more now. I'll see you Monday." He turned and walked away, and Steve and I quickly left the Foundation of Truth.

With plenty of time left before noon and our scheduled afternoon picnic trip, and since the day was warm and sunny, I talked Steve into stopping on the way to Stone Mountain at a do-it-yourself car wash and sprucing up my little Opel. We were almost done with the job, Steve had shut off the water and I was drying off the windows when the water somehow started again.

The pressurized hose began jumping and flailing wildly like a possessed snake, spraying water all over the car and me. I finally grabbed the hose, but not near enough the end to keep it from lashing me viciously about the head. On one of the blows, the metal hand grip belted me right across the mouth. I screamed and let go of the hose, which again flailed around free on the floor. Steve quickly shut the water off again and came walking toward me, laughing—until I took my hand away from my mouth.

I could tell by the look on his face I was hurt pretty bad. Whether from the blow or from shock, I didn't know which, my face had gone completely numb. But I tasted grit and blood, and with my tongue I could feel broken and loosened teeth.

Steve looked on the verge of panic. So I took charge and gave the orders. "You have to take me straight home," I told him. "I need to get this cleaned up and see how serious it is."

"Shouldn't we go to an emergency ward?" Steve asked.

I shook my head. "Take me home first." I didn't have any medical insurance, and I wasn't going to any hospital unless I was convinced there was no alternative.

But once we got in the car and Steve began to drive, I checked my mouth with the interior mirror. It looked worse than I'd imagined. "Take me to Dr. Peek's," I said, and I gave Steve the new directions. Dr. Peek had an M.D. friend in his building, and I knew he'd be glad to tell me whether or not I needed to go to the hospital.

But a few minutes later, when we reached the building, Dr. Peek's office was closed. So was the other doctor's. We'd returned to the car when I spotted another medical-looking sign. "What's that? Over there?" I pointed.

"It says D.D.S.," Steve reported.

"That's a dentist," I replied. "Let's go."

With my hand covering my mouth, I walked right into a waiting room, full of parents and children—obviously, a pediatric dentist's office. I kept right on walking into the work area and closed the door behind me. The receptionist-assistant looked up. When I took my hand away from my mouth, she turned white.

Before she could say a word, I blurted out an explanation. "I'm sorry about this, but I've been under terrible stress all week, my name is Sandy Purl, I was a stewardess in the plane crash that happened two years ago, and I just got hit in the mouth at a car wash, and I need the doctor to just look at me and tell me if I need to go to the hospital because I don't have any insurance."

I don't know how much she absorbed, but she ushered me to one of the examining rooms and told me to wait in the chair. A few minutes later, the dentist walked in.

"Hi, I'm Dr. Simon," he said. "Don't worry about anything, Sandy. We'll take care of you. Let's just see how things look here." And he began checking around my mouth.

I asked if I needed to go to a hospital. But he didn't think so. He washed out my gashes where my teeth had cut through just below my lip and said I could probably use a stitch or two, but he taped the cuts and said he thought that'd do. From what he said while he worked, it seemed obvious he knew all about my plane crash, probably from the news coverage earlier in the week. After cleaning up the inside of my mouth and examining my teeth, he said, "I suspect you're going to be very sore for a few days. Your facial bruises will last a couple of weeks. There's one, maybe two, teeth that may die within a couple years. If you come back Monday morning, I'll file down the front teeth that got chipped."

He told me to stay put and went to do something with a patient in another room. After he closed the door, the shock began to wear off and pain began to radiate out from my lips—up to my eyes, down to my chin, back to my ears. Like a searing flame, the pain quickly spread and throbbed through my entire face.

The moment I thought of the image of fire in connection with my face, I instantly flashed back to the crash. My mind resurrected memories that had never premiered in my conscious mind. I saw the hair and faces of passengers burst into flames and blister as the fire flooded the cabin. I saw blackened faces in the wreckage with eyes burned out of the sockets. Seeing the terror-filled, pain-filled faces of dying people, I imagined for the first time ever, the horrible burning pain some of my passengers had experienced for the last few seconds of their lives. Involuntarily, I screamed.

The doctor threw open the door to find me sobbing uncontrollably. He put his arms around me to comfort me until I regained enough composure to mumble an apology and try to explain that the pain in my face had sent me flashing back to all the burned and dead faces I'd seen in the crash.

I guess he understood, because he reached for a mirror and insisted that I look at my own face. "See?" he said. "No burns. You're going to be okay."

When I calmed down enough for him to feel he could leave again, he told me, "You can go anytime, Sandy. But you can stay here in the office the rest of the day if you need the time."

His words and his compassion prompted another outbreak of tears. But only a few more minutes passed before I felt ready to walk out of the office and ask Steve to take me on home.

Monday morning, on the way back to Dr. Simon's office, I stopped to pick up a small planter of flowers to give him and his staff as a small thank-you for their kindness to me. I jotted a quick little note to the doctor: "You were indeed an angel of mercy for someone in great need. May God bless you for your compassion and concern."

First I delivered the flowers to the dentist's office. Neither he nor his assistants could believe my face. The swelling had completely gone, without a hint of a bruise, and the cuts were healing nicely. Once Dr. Simon filed off my teeth, I looked as good as new. That (on top of the doctor's compassionate concern) was, for me, a providential sign, which sent me rushing home.

The minute I walked in the door, I went straight to the phone and called the Foundation of Truth. I told the secretary, "I had an accident over the weekend, and I won't be able to keep the appointment I had for a life reading this afternoon. No, I do not wish to reschedule the reading." When I hung up, I went to my room, gathered up some brochures I'd picked up at the psychic fair on

Saturday and dropped them in the kitchen trash. Then I tied up the kitchen trash bag, took it outside, and pitched it into the dumpster.

I'd been praying for some sort of answer, some sort of reassurance from God about my future. Now I had it. A neon sign couldn't have been any more obvious. I now saw a message in nearly everything that had happened to me since I'd walked into the psychic fair. The oppressive feel of the place, the uneasiness I felt. Even the minireading the psychic gave me; I could now see it had been so nonspecific and vague it could fit almost anyone. And then the freak accident in the car wash; it said to me, "What are you doing, Sandy? Where are you going?"

Dr. Simon's availability and mercy made me stop and wonder, "How many angels of mercy have crossed my path in the last two years?" I thought of the woman who had combed my hair at the scene of the crash. Then Laura, the neighbor who took me to the hospital in Denver the first time I blacked out. The encounter with Cheryl on that rooftop in Los Angeles, which forced me to realize I couldn't escape my past by running. Liz, encouraging me to look to God. The flight attendant on that flight to Washington, referring me to Del Mott, who put me in touch with Sandy Seagar. Mrs. Craton and the Newmans. My own sister Candy and her husband Larry. Dr. Peek. No, Dr. Simon was by no means the first angel on the scene. Time and again God had put the right person in my path at the right time. And that was the biggest answer I discovered that week: God has His own timing. And His timing is always better than mine.

I still didn't understand why this lesson had taken two years to learn. Maybe that was His timing, too. All I knew was I now felt more grateful about how far I'd come than worried about how far I had yet to go.

Chapter 16

Despite all I learned that week of the second anniversary, and despite the heartening progress I saw in myself, I can't say everything else went well that spring of 1979. I still harbored hard feelings against Southern Airways and some of the Southern staff. I continued to have to show my letter and explain myself every time I wanted to take a pass ride. And though I passed my five-year anniversary as a Southern Airways employee, I had to make numerous phone calls and do weeks of complaining to my union rep before the in-flight service department finally got around to sending me my five-year pin.

I'd experienced an even bigger hassle with Southern when they switched my monthly pay date without any prior notice. I had to wait for my worker's compensation, and I paid late charges on all my bills.

All these run-ins with Southern, big and small, had combined over two years to raise serious doubts in Sandy's mind that she could ever work for the company again. Fortunately, it now looked like she'd never have to. During that spring of 1979 Southern Airways and North Central Airlines were working out details for the merger of the two companies to form a new corporation—Republic Airlines.

So it was that at the end of April, when Sandy sent in her request for one more ninety-day extension on her medical leave, she knew it would be the last such request she'd ever have to make of the company she felt had deserted her. And she began to look to the birth of Republic as her chance for a new professional beginning for herself as well.

Dr. Peek and I felt I'd reached a new, solid plateau in my recovery climb. Early that summer we even agreed on a reasonable target date for my return to work—September 1. Sometimes I'd pull my little appointment calendar out of my purse and count the days to September 1. I saw that day as the final destination of what had often seemed a hopelessly long journey, and as the beginning of the rest of my life.

Sometime in June I received advance word of one more important stop in my journey to September. Del Mott, in her role as safety director for the Association of Flight Attendants, invited me to participate on a panel with other surviving flight attendants in Washington during August, as part of the AFA's Air Safety Training Seminar. I accepted with great excitement.

I'd already been able to share my experience with the people of New Hope and the city of Atlanta through the events and coverage of the second anniversary. And I'd shared the story of my spiritual pilgrimage with Youth for Christ and some churches that had asked me to speak. This panel, presented for flight attendants from around the country, would be my first opportunity to tell my whole story to professional colleagues—the people who most needed to be sensitized to the trauma of a crash's aftermath. This was a chance, perhaps, to make a difference in the airline industry. I now looked forward to the Washington seminar almost as much as my return to work.

Southern and North Central became Republic on the first of July. Later that month Sandy heard about yet another tragic airline disaster involving a Western Airlines jet in Mexico City. She immediately put in a call to talk with Del Mott. But she learned Del and another experienced counselor retained by the AFA had already been summoned by Western officials to counsel families and friends of those who died. Sandy wrote a letter of appreciation to Western's management for their sensitivity.

Also in July Dr. Peek agreed to go with Sandy in August and take part on the AFA panel. At the end of July, when her medical leave came near an end, Sandy and Dr. Peek agreed together to request only a thirty-day extension so she could begin work again as planned on September 1.

The summer sun was merciless the day I dropped by Dr. Peek's office to pick up my copies of the most recent correspondence. Standing in the waiting room, I read over his letters notifying Republic, the worker's compensation people, and my union of our request for another thirty days of medical leave. But there's no way to adequately express the joy I felt as I read these words:

Ms. Purl's level of emotional adjustment is most satisfactory at this time. A review of this case indicates she has made substantial progress since the referral in October 1978, and I am most pleased to advise that she will be able to return to work in the near future.

When I finished reading that paragraph, I danced around the waiting room as excited as an eight-year-old who'd just been given a birthday pony. Dr. Peek's secretary, whom I'd startled more than once by running distraughtly out of therapy, shared my joy by laughing along with me. And a few minutes later, after getting into my car in the parking lot, I read through the letters one more time before I started home. And all the way I kept telling myself, "I'm going back. I'm finally going back."

First came the seminar in Washington.

The AFA scheduled its Air Safety Training Seminar in a large meeting room of the George S. Meany Center. Dr. Peek and I sat in front with the rest of the panel—thirteen surviving flight attendants representing six different airlines and more than half a dozen separate crashes. We faced a roomful of about a hundred flight attendants, most of them base safety representatives such as I had been in Ft. Walton and New Orleans.

Margaret Barbeau, a psychiatric sociologist hired by the AFA, an experienced counselor to airline personnel and families of the dead after fatal plane crashes, moderated the meeting. She made a few opening remarks about our informal procedure, warned everyone in the room that the day promised to be emotionally intense, and advised that anyone experiencing strong reactions probably shouldn't leave the room without talking to someone about his or her feelings.

Preliminaries over with, three Alaskan Airline people spoke first. Two women and one man, they had all survived the same crash. The heavy silence blanketing the room as they talked was broken only by a scattered chorus of sniffling and noseblowing. My turn to speak came next.

Quickly and matter-of-factly I told my story. Beginning with the crash itself and then the crash scene, I brought the audience right up to date with my plans to go back to work the first of next month. I talked nonstop for over an hour.

I did slow down a few times when my voice broke, or to wipe tears out of my eyes. But I wasn't the only one crying.

Dr. Peek started talking as soon as I finished, retracing the eleven months of the story he'd been involved with. As he recounted my first visit and described my distressed condition, it seemed to me he was describing someone else—a stranger, perhaps. The longer he talked, the more I realized how much I'd changed. I was indeed a very different person from the Sandy of Los Angeles only a year before.

Once Dr. Peek wrapped up his comments, the rest of the panel told their stories. For some it was the first time they'd ever shared publicly. So the whole thing turned into a day-long therapy session—with spectators. An emotionally heavy day! By the time the panel concluded, the people attending that seminar had gained an unprecedented understanding of the traumatic aftermath of aviation disasters. And those of us who shared our stories came away with the undeniable assurance that at least twelve other human beings understood enough to empathize.

Not until several weeks later did I realize the true significance of what took place during that seminar. One day Candy's mail contained a large envelope addressed to me. I quickly tore it open to find a photocopy of a twenty-seven-page paper written by Margaret Barbeau, titled, "Responding to Mental Health Needs in Aircraft Disasters." Drawing on her own counseling experiences with crash survivors and focusing on the common reactions shared by the survivors who took part in the seminar, Margaret clearly described and defined an as-yet-unnamed postcrash reaction syndrome and suggested specific steps that people in the industry needed to take to provide immediate support and a better chance of long-term recovery for future victims, their families, and their associates.

Proudly I noted that Margaret's first page expressed appreciation by name for each of us who had participated in the special training seminar. As I began to read, I wept. *Where was this paper two years ago when I needed it?* But I soon realized I needed it even now. On those pages I found the words, the logic, and the intellectual rationale for the emotions and the illogical hysteria that had tormented me, that had *been* me, for so long. In those twenty-seven pages, I found self-understanding—at an astonishing new level.

I read that the degree of impact of an aircraft disaster on a victim

. . . is multidetermined, based on such factors as (1) the severity and nature of the disaster, (2) physical and psychological proximity to the event, (3) previous experience in personal crisis, and (4) the individual's life situation at the time of the event.

In my experience, (1) seventy-two people had died a terrifying death, (2) I not only lived through the crash, I stayed at the crash and subjected myself to another couple hours of unforgettable gore and trauma, (3) I had never properly, healthily processed my father's death, and (4) I'd been married less than a year, had moved just a few months before, and had been recently struggling with job-related fears. No wonder my life had fallen apart! With my characteristics, I was a prime candidate to become a basket case.

Barbeau went on to discuss common symptoms following the trauma of aircraft disasters. The list of typical psychological reactions read like a recent history of my own emotional life:

Psychic numbing, guilt, fear, phobias, mood swings, irritability and anger, rage, anxiety, depression, sadness, grief. Cognitive reactions noted included a lack of concentration, an inability to make decisions, impaired memory, and mental disorientation.

Barbeau cited common physical symptoms, including headaches, back pain, muscle spasms, gastrointestinal distress, lowered sexual energy, sleep disorders, nightmares, and skin rashes. Typical maladaptive behavioral reactions discussed in the paper included "abuse of alcohol," "displacing anger onto self and inappropriate others," "destroying relationships by provoking negative reactions," "withdrawal into isolation," "suicidal preoccupation or behavior," and "making impulsive major life changes."

That was me. All me. All those symptoms I'd feared for so long were proof of my insanity were typical of people who'd gone through experiences like mine. Far from crazy, I had so many of the "typical" symptoms you could have accurately called me "textbook typical."

And that self-understanding loosed an indescribable sense of soaring freedom. But insight didn't come without pain. That pain pierced deepest as I read these words:

Often the people closest to the victims—spouses, parents, lovers, children, intimate friends—have their own feelings of anger, fear, etc., and are less able to help with some needs. If the victim has expectations of these people which cannot be fulfilled, anger and alienation may ensue. Realistic expectations on the part of both people must include the disappointing reality that there are inherent limitations in these intimate relationships and that resources for help must include other people, too. Acceptance of this concept can help avoid some unnecessary strain and perhaps prevent a reactive termination of the relationship. Supportive counseling for both partners and families can be very helpful during and/or following the crisis phase.

"Oh, Mike," came my anguished inner cry. "If we'd only known! What a difference this one paper could have made. If it's too late for us, thank God it's not too late for any survivors to come."

Indeed, the last fourteen pages of the paper offered detailed guidelines as to how flight attendants and others in the airline industry could assist and support any future disaster victims. I read those recommendations without the emotional reactions I'd felt in the first half of the paper. "Never again," I told myself, "will another surviving flight attendant have to wander and wonder alone. Never again."

Meantime, at the end of August, Sandy received a summons to travel to Republic headquarters in Minneapolis for a psychological and physical exam by company-selected doctors to determine her suitability for active duty. After a couple thorough examinations, the doctors gave her the go-ahead to begin working again as soon as Republic called her after September 1.

One of the flight attendants who shared on the safety training panel with Sandy had been a North Central crew member in a nonfatal crash in Kalamazoo, Michigan. When Connie Anderson had heard the account of Southern's corporate attitude toward Sandy, she'd assured Sandy, "The people at Republic will be different. You'll see." And in-

deed, if her first experience with Republic's offices in Minneapolis were any indication, Connie had been right. Sandy headed home very grateful for the merger.

Standing at the airport gate, waiting for my flight out of Minneapolis, I spotted a familiar face among the waiting passengers. Although I knew I'd seen the man at Southern headquarters in Atlanta, I didn't think we'd ever met. Yet he registered recognition and surprise when he saw me, so he obviously knew who I was.

I smiled and said hello.

"What are you doing in Minneapolis?" he asked.

Trying to keep the conversation light and casual, I replied, "I just came up to let some shrinks suck on my brain a while before I can start back to work."

Again he registered surprise and glanced furtively around as if concerned about who might have heard my remark. And that was pretty much the end of our conversation before we boarded the plane. We changed flights in Memphis, and I pointed the man out to one of the flight attendants I knew. When she told me his name, I gasped.

He was the same Southern executive who'd refused my request for reimbursement of my personal items lost in the crash. The same man who had called me again and again to demand to know, "What is it you expect from us?"

Knowing he had been the perpetrator of what I felt had been the most direct harassment I'd had from Southern, I avoided the man on the flight to Atlanta. But once we'd deplaned at Hartsfield International, I passed him in the terminal and he stopped me. "Sandy," he said, "I just want you to know that the same people who were making decisions about you with Southern are making the decisions for Republic."

I couldn't believe my ears. And I didn't trust my tongue. So I turned and walked away without saying a word.

What should have been a joyous homecoming full of anticipation had turned to a night of discouragement and dread. The next day was September 1.

Chapter 17

For the next couple of weeks, Sandy stewed and fretted about what would happen when the airline called her back on active duty. But no calls came, so she remained on worker's compensation. However, the longer the delay and the more she thought about the Southern executive she'd encountered on the trip back from Minneapolis, the angrier she became.

She finally determined to quit worrying and complained to her union representative, who became indignant at what she heard. The rep promised to take Sandy's case directly to a Republic vice-president she felt certain would respond fairly. "The union will stand behind you on this one, Sandy," the representative said. "You can count on us."

Indeed, when the vice-president heard an account of Sandy's experience and read the new research paper by Margaret Barbeau on the recommended response to victims of aircraft disasters, he became angry at the treatment Sandy had gotten from Southern and immediately reinstated her medical insurance as a gesture of fairness and good faith. He promised Sandy would have every chance she needed to be successfully reintegrated in the new company. By the time this executive handed down the word on Sandy to middle management, the required recurrent training time for September had passed. But before the month was out, Minneapolis notified Sandy she would take her recurrent training in October and begin flying again in November.

Recurrent training proved easier than I'd imagined. The four years I'd spent on the job had taught me well. Everything seemed to have stuck. The only rough spot for me was the emergency crash procedure. As part of that coverage we watched movies about two different crashes. The first included remarkable footage of an actual crash shot from inside the cabin. The crash had occurred many years before in Japan. One of the passengers had filmed the whole thing on his home movie camera. We watched the flight attendant give her emergency briefing, including instruction on how to open the emergency window exits. We saw the violent bounce of impact and the overhead baggage flying around the cabin before the plane came to a stop. Then we watched as the passengers by the window exits opened the exits, exactly as they'd been instructed. Then most of the class broke into laughter when the men who had removed the window exits lined up in the aisle and waited for someone to open the regular door before they filed out to safety. It seems the stewardess had neglected to say the obvious—that once the emergency exits were open, passengers were to use them.

The film reminded me once again of the responsibility of the job and the absolute trust passengers place in the crew during emergencies. I thought back to that flight soon after I'd begun to fly when the cabin had depressurized and every single passenger had unquestioningly and instantly obeyed my absurdly jumbled instructions. That too had seemed funny at the time. But now I also thought of the frightened, questioning eyes of those passengers on Flight 242. I remembered their rapt attention and careful obedience to all I said in my emergency briefing. And I couldn't laugh at that old Japanese film.

The second movie told the story of North Central's Kalamazoo crash, the one Connie Anderson had survived. The instructor introduced it as the "happy crash" because no one had died. But as the camera panned the crash site, I had to fight the urge to run from the room or at least scream, "There's no such thing as a happy crash!" Connie's crash had happened a couple years before; but she still wasn't back to work.

I said nothing. But silent tears trickled slowly down my cheeks as I closed my eyes and awaited the end of the movie. Sitting next to me on the very front row of the class sat my good friend Donna Alleman, who'd stayed with me in the hospital after the crash. She just happened to be taking recurrent training at the same time. When she looked over and noticed my tears, she jotted a quick note and slipped it in front of me where I could read, "Don't let anyone else know what's happening." I nodded a little acknowledgment. I didn't want anyone questioning my emotional control. Since everyone else sat behind us, no one else ever knew.

Once I'd completed my classroom work, I awaited only one final prescribed step before I could officially begin work. The on-line check. I was to show up at the airport the morning of October 31; my supervisor would select a flight for me to work with a regularly scheduled crew, and the supervisor would ride the flight to observe and grade my performance.

In recent months, Dr. Peek and I had talked a lot about my impending return to work. As the date drew closer, he talked me through the regular procedures and even assigned me some desensitization exercises in which I acted out all the steps of preparation I routinely go through before a flight. He even went so far as to have me pack my bag as I do the night before a trip and then drive to the airport the next morning, imagining I was going to take a real flight.

The roleplaying seemed to have helped; as I set everything out on the night of the thirtieth, my actions felt familiar and routine. It didn't feel so much like a major emotional first.

However, the morning of the thirty-first was another story. I'd not yet been issued a new Republic uniform; I'd had to borrow one from my supervisor. So dressing and seeing myself in official flight garb was an unavoidable and difficult first. Standing in my bedroom, checking the fit in the mirror, I realized as never before what that uniform meant. I doubted I could ever put one on again without feeling an awesome weight of responsibility. As I stood and looked at my "official" self, in my mind I once again saw all those helpless, trusting eyes of my passengers, looking to me as their authority, their savior. I'd failed so many of them.

I can't even remember now where my on-line check flight went. I do remember I walked ahead of the rest of the crew as we crossed the concrete between the terminal and the waiting DC-9. First to the steps, I led the single-file procession onto the plane. I desperately wanted to stop at the top of the stairs and take a deep breath before entering. But feeling the pressure of my peers quickly mounting the steps behind me, I went, without a pause, through the door and turned right past the galley. As I carried my flight bag down the cabin aisle, I felt a deep, instinctual urge to turn and run. Perhaps I *would* have run if the captain, co-captain, the two regular flight attendants, and my supervisors hadn't been right behind me blocking the way.

For a few moments I almost panicked. "Sandy, you can't turn back now!" I lectured myself. "You've come too far." But the fear and frustration welled up and spilled out in tears.

"Don't stop now. Don't even turn around, Sandy. You can't let this stop you." I strode the full length of the cabin and stepped right into the rear bathroom to wash my face and regain my composure. Moments later I emerged, my secret emotions tightly reined.

After takeoff, when I joined the other flight attendants in the galley to prepare to serve the passengers, I began to shake. I knew the other girls were watching me, so I forced a smile and tried to reassure them: "I'm going to be all right. Please understand, this is just a first for me."

What really bothered me wasn't the flight, but the fear that I was going to lose control, do something dumb, or forget something essential in front of my supervisor and thus fail my official check. And the thought of messing up now, after waiting so long, set my hands shaking so bad I thought I wasn't going to be able to pour the coffee. So I gave myself a little lecture: "What are you doing, Sandy? You *know* this job. You did it for four whole years. And you performed your duty under the worst possible situation. Just do your job!"

And that's what I did. When I returned to the galley with an empty coffee pot, the other girls grinned their congratulations; they were rooting for me. And I responded with a short celebratory dance step.

That was the pattern for the rest of the flight. After each completed duty, we'd meet back in the galley, and they'd give me friendly hugs, pats, or encouraging words. And my confidence soared as each task just got easier and easier.

The biggest test of the day came on the first landing. As I took my too-familiar place in the B-position jumpseat, I began to sweat.

Wiping the perspiration from my face, I also felt short of breath; instinctively I leaned forward and put my head between my knees to get some relief. Then the thought suddenly struck, "Oh, no! This is the brace position!" I jerked myself upright again to ride out what proved to be a fairly smooth landing. From then on, I knew I had it made.

Back in Atlanta after the trip, the supervisor subjected me to a two-hour debriefing quiz instead of the routine 20-minute exam I'd gotten on my first on-line check with Southern. She must have asked me every first aid and procedural question she could think of before we finished. When it was over, I received "Excellent" marks on everything.

Thinking "This deserves a toast!" I stopped for a couple of cans of Tab on the way and took them by Dr. Peek's office. He laughed and shared my victory.

The very next day I took my first working trip. Almost all the nervousness of the preceding day had disappeared. I flew the New York run with a full plane. The other flight attendant, an eighteen-year Southern veteran, and I had so much work to do I didn't have time to think, let alone worry. By the time I returned to Atlanta that afternoon, I looked haggard and felt sore muscles I'd forgotten I had.

After the passengers deplaned and we'd hurriedly cleaned up the plane before the next crew came on, the girl working with me squeezed my arm and said, "I'm so proud of you, Sandy. You've really got yourself together." Those words soothed away all the aches and sent me from the plane tired but happy.

Before I could even get from the plane to the terminal, a cousin of mine who works at the airport vaulted a little maintenance fence and ran to greet me with long-stemmed red roses. Candy and Larry met me inside. Everyone looked so proud—almost as proud as I felt to realize, "I'm back. I'm finally back!"

I experienced a number of other firsts during November and December—the first mechanical delay of a flight, the first storm. But while I could feel my tension level climb a few steps, I coped and did my job without faltering.

Campus Life magazine published a long, two-part account of my two-and-a-half-year ordeal that proved more therapeutic than I could have imagined. For the first time, through that story, which I could hand to a few of my close friends, I was finally able to share many of the painful, personal details of my experience—in a nonthreatening, unemotional way. Seeing my own story in black and white gave me an unexpected sense of objective distance about what I'd been through; the permanence of print provided a sense of finality to the experience.

And when the November 19, 1979, issue of *Time* magazine reported on the Air Safety Training Seminar we'd held in August, leading with a summary of my story and running my picture with the report, I felt there was nothing left to hide. *Time's* biggest story of the week was the Iranian takeover of the U.S. embassy in Tehran. But I knew virtually everyone in the airline industry would have seen or heard about the *Time* article about the seminar. And that meant they would have heard about the panel of surviving flight attendants and would at least realize I wasn't alone in my experience or my reactions.

I particularly hoped everyone who saw the article would remember the quote from Margaret Barbeau, the seminar leader, who assured *Time*, "You can walk away from an accident without physical injury. But the emotional injury may be even worse. You can't x-ray it, but the injuries are real." I very much wanted my colleagues to hear that, to realize I wasn't crazy, and to understand why I'd taken so long to return to work. And what better way for them to hear it than from the pages of *Time* magazine the very month I came back to work. I thanked God for that bit of perfect timing. Everything seemed to be working together for my easiest possible reintegration into work.

Each of my first three months, I had bid for the easiest trips I could find. Flight attendants' schedules change every month. So as part of the industry-wide monthly ritual, every crew member, pilots as well as flight attendants, at each flight base puts in a request, usually called a bid, for preferred trip schedules. You rank your list of desired trips in order of preference. The number of choices you have to make depends on your seniority. Since there were about sixty flight attendants in Atlanta who were ahead of me in seniority, I had to bid for sixty-some possible schedules. Then management assigns the crews for the entire month based on the combination of bids and seniority. Naturally, those at the top of the seniority list usually bid for the trips to the most interesting cities or for the longest flights.

Every flight attendant has to log a certain number of flying hours each month. And the longer flights not only knock off those hours more quickly, but they're easier work. One 3-hour flight requires one check-in, one boarding, one set of passengers to serve, one deboarding, and one clean-up, while three 1-hour flights mean three of everything—almost three times as much work. The best trips in each crew base might require only two or three days a week of flying, while the worst trips would take four or five days a week to accumulate the required monthly hours.

So I'd been bidding for trips solely on the basis of fewest take-offs and landings. I didn't care where I flew, or where I spent any overnights. All that mattered to me was getting the fewest individual flights, because I wanted to ease back into flying as gently as possible and I felt it was the number of up-and-downs that would add to any strain I might feel. Because I had enough seniority among the Atlanta-based flight attendants, I was able to get what I figured would be the least strenuous flights in November and December.

My January schedule also looked good, with only four up-and-downs a day. But my cautious plan broke down halfway through the month when Republic announced a systemwide schedule change. In the middle of what had seemed would be a very easy flying month, everyone's trips were juggled and I found myself flying an exhausting 2-day trip with thirteen takeoffs and landings a day. While four flights a day had seemed a manageable routine, I quickly found there was nothing routine about thirteen flights and 1,300 passengers to greet and serve in one long shift.

I don't have the foggiest memory of where we flew or where we spent the night on that first grueling trip. And the second day, with each taxi-out, each passenger briefing, and each time I had to point out the emergency exits to a cabinful of new faces, I could feel the tension level, like a river at flood stage, steadily rising. By afternoon, every takeoff and landing set off a severe case of shakes, and I had to breathe deeply and force steadiness on my voice every time I spoke to a passenger. The feelings threatened to flood through at any moment, and I felt as if I'd used up all the sandbags in my reserve. When the trip finally ended that night in Atlanta, I literally staggered off the plane.

I'd been trying to ease out of Candy's and Larry's lives and give them as much privacy as I could. For that reason I'd planned to stay that night at the apartment of a friend who was out of town. But it wasn't the best night to be alone, because I no sooner entered that empty apartment than the terrible thoughts hit me: "Sandy, you've got to go back early tomorrow morning and fly the same two-day trip all over again. And you can't do it."

At first I told myself I'd feel better after a good night's rest. I couldn't even begin to sleep. About midnight I made my first trip to the bathroom and vomited up blood. After a couple more bathroom visits, I tried to reach someone in Atlanta operations to tell them they'd have to replace me on the morning flight. When I couldn't reach anyone in Atlanta, I tried headquarters in Minneapolis. No answer.

I didn't have my supervisor's home number, so I had to keep calling the Atlanta and Minneapolis offices through the night. Finally I got through to the operations office in Minneapolis sometime between 5 and 6 A.M., only an hour or so before I was scheduled to report. I told them I was having anxiety problems, and they'd have to replace me. When I hung up, I finally went back to bed and slept till afternoon.

After all I'd been through, I was back on medical leave.

Chapter 18

In the next few days I tried to convince management at Republic that I could go back on the line if I could just fly part-time. I'd been coping so well for two-and-a-half months. I knew I'd be okay if I only didn't have to work a full, heavy schedule. But my supervisor informed me federal regulations wouldn't allow me to come back gradually.

When Sandy failed to make any headway, Dr. Peek appealed to the airline on her behalf. In a letter dated January 23, 1980, he wrote: (Sandy Purl) "has been seen in therapy on several occasions in the past 10 days. At this time she is experiencing a somatization disorder with abdominal pain and vomiting. This condition appears to be associated with a direct reaction to increased anxiety. There has been consider-able stabilization in the (past) treatment of the (patient's) post trau-matic stress disorder, to the extent that regular therapy had been dis-continued. . . . . It is my opinion the current disorder results from two ongoing processes. The first is the moderate amount of regression often anticipated in the resolution of this type of disorder. The second factor and probably the most important in this case is the accelerated rate at which she has returned to former work settings. Her return to flying should be at a more gradual rate in order to increase the likelihood that she would not experience recurrent episodes of uncontrollable anxiety. Overall her general response and adjustment has been satis-factory and the present condition is seen as a temporary adjustment problem."

Sandy's supervisor wrote back on February 13 to thank Dr. Peek for his letter, to express ongoing concern for Sandy's health and to explain in part: ". . . Unfortunately, Federal Air Regulations state that all crew members must be fully qualified with no limitations, and because of the nature of the job it is impossible for Sandy to return to work at a much more gradual rate as you so stated in your letter. Until Sandy fully recovers from the recent post traumatic stress disorder, I cannot permit her to return to active flight status and shall consider her on Medical Leave of Absence until further correspondence from you is received."

So it was all or nothing. I was back to Square One. In contrast to the preceding months when I'd been flying as high emotionally as I had literally, this new discouragement seemed like an all-time low. I'd been celebrating my return by telling every friend I'd seen since November 1. Now I had to explain my new status—or, more accurately, my nonstatus—to everyone who inquired.

What made this even worse was the fact that I could no longer blame the airline. Republic had been good to me. They'd brought me back, and many Republic people had been supportive and encouraging. So I couldn't rationalize away or pass the blame onto a company this time. This failure was a personal failure. This time the problem was all mine. And that truth was as bitter to accept for myself as it was to admit to others.

But in soon being able to admit it to Dr. Peek, I came also to accept the problem and the implications—the biggest, most important of which was that I had to take full responsibility for my own life. I could no longer keep saying, "The airline needs to do this or that. They really ought to be doing something for me." It was time to make my own decisions about my own future.

That was just one of the things we talked about in therapy over the next few weeks. While I wasn't ready to give up the hope that I would resume flying again someday, Dr. Peek and I agreed on the value of considering alternative careers. That was one reason I enrolled for the spring term at Georgia State University in downtown Atlanta.

There were additional reasons. I remembered how therapeutic school had been for me in Denver, how it not only had filled my time and my mind, but also had provided an arena of success to bolster my self-confidence. I needed that sort of relief again.

School would provide another benefit. It'd offer needed practice in reintegrating into groups of people, a necessary skill no matter what I did in the future. So I signed up for two basic undergraduate classes. Biology—because I maintained a serious interest in the nursing or some medically related career. And psychology—because I now had a strong personal appreciation for that discipline.

But school didn't turn out to be the same sort of distraction it'd been in Denver. Much of what we studied in psychology very naturally made me rethink my own experiences and emotions. So although I found it interesting and at times even helpful in understanding myself, the class wasn't exactly the place to escape from my problems. To my initial, but short-lived horror, our text even included a picture of the PSA crash in San Diego, accompanying a brief discussion of transient disorders—which, it said, commonly follow such disasters.

I didn't say a word in class the day we covered that chapter. No one knew, except my professor. The couple of times I shared a little with her about my experience, she was extremely warm and supportive.

Surprisingly, biology proved the more disturbing of the two classes. I'd always loved biology and made excellent grades in all the science classes I'd had through school. I enjoyed this one, too—for a while. Then came the day in class, during a unit on human anatomy, that the professor announced we'd be leaving the classroom and going up to a lab on one of the upper floors to observe a cadaver.

I swallowed hard and looked around to see the mixed reactions on the faces of the other students in my class. I hadn't counted on this.

I screwed up all the courage I could and followed the professor and the others out of the class and up the stairs. I toyed with the idea of slipping quietly away down the stairwell. Instead, I followed meekly along like a helpless sheep. Moments later, we walked out into an upstairs hallway for a short walk before the lead members of the group began filing into a room.

As I approached the doorway, I stopped and looked in. There on a lab table I saw not only a human corpse, but beside it, a severed arm and leg. I shrieked. And then, covering my mouth with my hand to contain my lunch, I turned and ran as fast as I could down the hall to the nearest bathroom. "No one," I told myself, "No one should ever have to look at pieces of human bodies."

I finished the term with a D in biology. Despite the A grade earned in psychology, I decided not to enroll for the summer quarter.

I did, however, take another major step toward reassuming full responsibility for my own life. That spring I rented an apartment of my own. I couldn't afford much on my worker's compensation pay. But after searching and searching I found a rundown complex renting one-bedroom apartments for $140 a month. I had to admit even at that rent the place looked way overpriced. The painted trim on the outside of the apartments was cracked and peeling. Sheets of plywood covered a few of the windows in other apartments around the complex. Knee-high grass and weeds next to the buildings added to the neglected, almost deserted look.

I spent weeks scrubbing and painting before I moved my hodge-podge of boxes and garage sale belongings into the place. Then, for a long time, I'd go to the apartment to spend my days and feel a measure of independence, then go back to Candy's or some friend's to sleep. I just didn't want to be alone. When, after several weeks of living in two places, I finally made the break, I discovered a wonderful sense of self-reliance and confidence in finally being on my own.

In many ways I lived in a sort of limbo. I was constantly broke, residing alone in a rat-trap apartment that was little more than a lousy motel room with an outdated kitchen, and without a clue as to where I was going, career-wise. But I was coping and surviving on my own. As the months dragged by, that alone seemed heartening progress.

October brought with it another ego-boosting experience when the flight attendant's union in Australia flew me to Sydney to take part in a major training program to sensitize Qantas personnel to the aftereffects of an aircraft disaster. One of the Australian union officials had attended the Washington seminar over a year earlier and had gone home convinced something needed to be done to educate her national airline industry. When she'd worked out the details, she invited me, along with the three Alaskan Airline flight attendants who'd been in Washington, to come and share our experiences.

The Australian trip that resulted became a turning point for me. The first day of the seminar I met not only scores of flight attendants who served as safety representatives, but I met a number of pilots and even more officials representing the management structure of Qantas Airlines. When I stood in front of that crowd of 250 people and told my story, many were moved to tears. But I particularly noted the reaction of the company executives, the compassion and empathy I read in their eyes as I talked about the insensitivity and the ostracism I had felt from my company. "Obviously," I thought to myself, even as I talked, "here is a company with a management that cares. Look at these men and women wanting to understand what they can do in response and support when their company experiences a fatal crash. This is wonderful."

But then a new truth dawned. "These officials had come because they wanted to understand. But before today they didn't have any more idea about what psychological reactions to expect or how to respond than Southern's management had three and a half years before." I finally understood that the people at Southern hadn't had a vendetta against me. They hadn't been out to get Sandy Purl. They just hadn't known what to expect or how to react.

The other major impact of my Australian experience was the satisfaction I received from being able to play a small part in a precedent-setting event in the international airline industry. Flight attendants, pilots, and union and airline management officials had banded together for four days to learn how to most successfully deal with a crucial, but previously overlooked, issue.

I returned from "Down Under" so motivated that I began to bug Republic about finding me a job in another department. My union's contract compelled the company to try to train any disabled flight attendants for another position. And indeed, Dr. Peek had written management requesting such a move back in the summer, and one of the executives had promised to pursue that course of action for me. But so far, nothing had transpired.

Now that I'd had such a positive experience in Australia, I was itching to do something, to contribute and earn my way doing something. So I called and got the union working to see that something happened. Soon management informed me I could begin official training in Minnesota with the next class of reservations agents right after the first of the year.

So, January 11, 1981, I began my first official step toward career rehabilitation. When I graduated from training two weeks later, I went to work full-time in Atlanta as a Republic Airlines reservations agent. As an employee of a whole new department, I started at the very bottom of the seniority totem pole. I worked longer hours, and the pay only amounted to two-thirds of what I'd been making as a flight attendant. But I was working again and, by virtue of my old union contract, I had a full twelve months before the company could drop me from the ranks of flight attendants; as long as I qualified medically, I could return to flying at any time before the year was up. So my options remained open.

On February 4, one of F. Lee Bailey's staff attorneys called: "There's a new federal judge assigned to the unsettled cases resulting from your crash. He wants to settle this thing soon, and he's set a trial date for February 23.

"Everyone wants to settle out of court," the attorney said. "But you have to tell me how much money you need out of this."

I told him there was no amount of money that could compensate for everything I'd lost and gone through. But at the same time I wouldn't trade everything I'd learned, everything I'd gained for any amount of money. So I found it difficult to try to put any kind of a dollar sign on what I'd experienced in the aftermath of the crash.

He said he understood that. "But we've got to have a figure."

I'd already added up my lost income, estimated the losses I suffered in liquidating all my possessions, and tried to roughly estimate the cost of returning to my previous lifestyle. But there was no way I figured I'd get that much. So I threw out a much lower figure. The lawyer added a third to that amount. "I don't think we should settle for anything less." I knew the lawyers would get a third, I'd have to repay worker's compensation, and there was a small pile of other bills I'd accumulated. So there would be little or nothing left, but I didn't figure we'd get any more. And neither did the lawyer.

He called back with the defendants' first offer a couple days later.

I told him, "If that's all they're offering, I'd rather they just give the money to some church or orphanage where it would do some good. Let's just go to court." I was ready to put my trust in the American judicial system.

"But we don't stand a chance in court," the lawyer argued. "You worked for the airline, which is one of the parties of the suit. The judge won't look favorably upon that." He went on to explain that the liability trial, to determine which parties were responsible for what, would take weeks and cost $50–70,000 by the time all the experts finished testifying. Then there would have to be a separate trial on damages after, and if, liability could be established. "If you lost, you'd be stuck with paying the trial costs."

"At least I'd have a chance to tell my story where it had a chance of making a difference," I said. My lawyer told me he didn't think the courts were the best arena for crusading for the rights of future victims. But I told him, "I'm ready to take my chances."

He told me if I felt that way, he'd better go back and see if the opposition would make a better offer. And they did increase their offer. Two times. I turned them both down. The closer we got to the date of the trial, the more certain I felt that if justice was truly blind and fair, a court might well reach a decision that could help force some reform in the way the industry deals with crash survivors.

However, the closer we got to the trial, the more alarmed the attorneys for all the defendants became. They didn't want to go through the time and the expense of a trial any more than my lawyers did. So, with only a couple days left before the trial was to begin, they contacted my lawyers with a surprising proposal.

"I don't believe it," my lawyer said, when he called me. "But the other side says they'll waive liability, if we'll waive the right to a jury and just let the judge hear the case for damages." He went on to explain this meant the defendants had decided to somehow share the payment of any damages and that we'd all avoid the long and costly liability trial. But it also meant we wouldn't be able to appeal to the compassion of a jury.

My lawyer felt the offer was the best break we could hope for and recommended I accept it. So I agreed.

The case went to trial as scheduled on February 23, 1981, my twenty-eighth birthday. Candy and I arrived early and sat down to wait. I read a couple of pages from a prayer book I'd gotten at church and then I offered a short, silent prayer asking God for the strength to make it through the trial.

Mike and his lawyer were in attendance. He'd sued separately for loss of consortion in the breakup of our marriage. And my trial would therefore determine any damages he received as well.

When all the principals had arrived and the bailiff entered the courtroom, I hurried to my place at the table with my trial lawyer. We all stood for the judge to enter, and when we were seated once again the bailiff announced the case in a ringing voice: "Sandy Purl versus the United States of America."

Those words sent shivers of revulsion coursing through me. I wanted to shout: "Wait a minute. There's been some mistake." As those words, "Sandy Purl versus the United States of America," seemed to echo forever from those courtroom walls, I could see my father in his Air Force uniform spinning in his grave. I knew the U.S. Weather Service and the FAA were two of the defendants, but there were others as well. I wasn't intending to challenge my country.

I glanced back at Candy and saw she had turned white as a sheet. And I knew she was thinking the same thought I was: "What chance do I have suing the U.S. government in a federal court where a federal judge has the sole and final deciding word?"

I felt like a little ol' country girl getting taken for a ride in the big city. All I wanted to do was get out and go home.

My confidence wasn't helped any when the defending lawyers

spent their entire opening remarks stating and restating their contention that while their clients may have waived liability they still weren't really liable for any of my alleged damages.

Candy became the first witness to testify. My lawyer used her to establish a basic chronology of events and to detail for the court the emotional trauma and evident psychological disturbances I had experienced. Dr. Peek testified second about both my problems and my progress. A union representative testified about a number of job-related questions and my conflicts with my company. Then I testified and covered all the old ground once again, some of it more than once. Mike testified last.

The defendants tried to discount the connection of my emotional and psychological problems to the crash. They insisted the fact that I'd undergone hypnosis for a fear of flying just a few months before the crash meant that everything that had happened afterward stemmed from a pre-existing condition. They pointed to the divorce and argued that was reason in itself for great distress. They dredged up the abortion and insisted that was possibly the primary source of my distress. They even insinuated that the baby hadn't been Mike's; I thought Candy was going to jump up and clobber the lawyer at that point.

Testimony and cross examination went on for four days. By the time all the witnesses had been called, I felt as if someone had detonated a bomb inside me. My marriage, my emotional health, my entire life had been blown apart, and the pieces strewn around that courtroom for everyone to see.

No sooner had the attorneys summed up their arguments than the judge paused, looked down at his notes, and asked, "Is everyone ready?"

"For what? What's he doing?" I whispered to my lawyer. I was certain I had missed something; I just knew the judge was going to have to wrestle for hours with his decision because it was going to have such an impact on my life, on an entire industry. "What's happening?" I asked my lawyer again.

"Shhhh," he whispered back. "The judge has made his decision."

"He's what?"

"Just be quiet. And wait here."

The judge called the lawyers for all parties to the bench and half a dozen men walked forward. Then he reminded everyone that his decision would be sealed and all parties were sworn to secrecy and bound by law not to reveal the details of this settlement until all remaining cases stemming from the crash had been closed. This meant I couldn't even tell Candy.

Finally the judge wrote something on a tablet of paper and turned it so the lawyers could read it. Each of the men began frantically scribbling on his own paper. My lawyer returned to the table, and when everyone else had again been seated, he stood and said, "Though I can't completely agree with the amount of the settlement, I would like to thank the court on behalf of my client."

When he had finished his statement, the judge adjourned the court. No sooner had the gavel hit the bench than my head hit the table as I slumped forward in exhaustion and relief. "It's finally over. I don't care that we lost. I told my story and it's finally over." And my entire mind focused on the refreshing feel of the cool surface of the table against my flushed and sweaty forehead. But the next instant my lawyer tried to shove a piece of paper under my nose. "Did you see this? Sandy, look at this! Did you see?"

I slowly lifted my head and tried to focus my eyes on the figures scrawled across his paper. "There has to be some mistake," I thought. "That's even more than I had said I'd settle for." I gave my lawyer a giant bear hug and simultaneously wondered how I could keep from telling Candy.

What seemed like such a huge settlement quickly shrunk. Once the lawyers took their third and Sandy repaid the other bills and debts she'd accumulated during almost four years of unemployment, a sizable chunk of the money was gone. Yet what remained was enough to replace some of the furniture and belongings she'd sold and begin thinking of putting the rest toward some place to live—maybe a small condo in Atlanta.

Not until several days after the trial concluded did I realize how heavily the lawsuit must have been weighing on me. It wasn't as if

I had spent long hours brooding about it; weeks and months had sometimes gone by without any progress or contact from the lawyers. But looking back, I began to sense that I must have stored a big, heavy "unfinished" trunk of emotions somewhere in the corner of my subconscious that I had to drag with me everywhere I went. Because now that the trial was over, I experienced a wonderful sensation of unfettered energy.

I felt so good I decided not to go back to work at flight reservations. Instead I put my name in to go back on the line again as a flight attendant. "It's now or never," I told myself. "If I still can't handle the pressures of the job, I need to find out once and for all. The time has come to put the crash behind me and get on with my life."

Chapter 19

On April 1, 1981, three days short of the four-year anniversary of the crash, I went back on the line again, on reserve status. Flying reserve meant I didn't have a regular monthly schedule; instead, I'd fill in for people who called in sick or couldn't make a flight because of delays or whatever. My thought was that I'd be able to ease back in without having to fly a tough monthly schedule. What I hadn't counted on was the emotional strain of having to be prepared to fly on a moment's notice.

That strain began to multiply as the days went by without a call to fly. Every day I'd get out of bed and try to psych myself up to be ready to fly my first trip in fourteen months. Each time the phone rang, I'd jump up wondering, "Is this it?" Each night I'd go to bed drained by the tension. In my closet hung my brand-new uniform with the price tags still dangling from it; I couldn't quite bring myself to cut them off. By the second week of the month, the daily uncertainty began to trigger some all-too-familiar anxiety symptoms. My hands would shake and my stomach hurt. Periodically I'd cry, out of frustration and dread that the call would come and I wouldn't be able to pull myself together in time to make the flight and do my job.

I knew, deep down inside, that this would have to be my last shot at being a flight attendant. Despite all the excitement and positive emotional energy I'd gained in the preceding few weeks, I now felt all the old doubts creeping back in. A couple of times I became so distressed that Dr. Peek came to my place to help settle me down. Finally I called my new supervisor, a woman I didn't really know, to say I was experiencing a lot of anxiety about my return to work.

The new supervisor responded wonderfully. "Come on out to the airport," she said. "We'll have lunch and we can talk."

When I told her about the tension and uncertainty I'd been suffering through for almost two weeks, she didn't act the least bit alarmed. Her response was the most understanding reaction I could have imagined. "After what you've been through," she assured me, "your feelings sound perfectly normal to me." As a practical solution for the continuing, difficult uncertainty, she told me she'd look over her trip and personnel lists and schedule a first flight she could tell me about ahead of time. "Then you won't have to sit by the phone wondering and worrying."

So that's what we did. My supervisor scheduled me on an upcoming trip to Washington. I got myself ready emotionally, and my first flight back went without a hitch. After flying a few more flights on reserve, I went back on a regular monthly schedule the first of May.

My friends told me later that I was a little anxious to start with. One girlfriend laughed and said, "I remember on takeoff your body would tense, and you'd reach over and squeeze my hand or my knee." I don't remember any of that. For me, the return went smoother and easier than I could have ever imagined.

Time after time, in those first months back, I was reminded of why I loved my job, why I'd waited and hoped for so long to go back. Flight attendants receive so many rewards from the people they serve, and I'd missed that. I'd missed the genuine gratitude in the eyes of an eighty-five-year-old woman after you help her with her coat and slowly escort her up the jetway to meet her grandchildren. Or the heartfelt "Thank you!" of a harried young mother when you volunteer to take her foldup stroller, her diaper bag, and her impatient, rambunctious three-year-old and accompany her into the gate so she can concentrate her attention on her crying newborn baby. Or the inner satisfaction of knowing you've made the end of a long, hard-working day a little more cheerful and pleasant for a plane-load of tired commuting businesspeople.

In my four years of flying before the crash, I'd always enjoyed the interaction, the serving of my passengers. I had often come home from a trip emotionally drained by the constant demands of the people I met.

Now, however, I seemed to have more emotional energy to

give. I discovered an amazing and wonderful secret. The more I invested, the more I gave to the people I encountered, the more love and energy God gave me to give.

One day, not long after my return to work, our flight began pulling away from the terminal at Washington Dulles when we got called back to the gate. A messenger came aboard for one of our woman passengers to inform her that her mother had just died. The pilots held the plane while the lady reentered the terminal to take a phone call telling her the details. I went with her to provide any support I could.

In shock after the call, she couldn't decide whether to continue her flight to Atlanta or stay and try to get a direct flight home to Tuscaloosa from Washington. I explained she could make a better connection from Atlanta, so we reboarded the plane and took off. I had a full plane to serve, yet I wanted to reach out to this poor woman. So in the galley, preparing the cart of drinks, I just paused a moment and prayed, "Lord, that woman needs comfort. But I don't have time to give it right now. You'll have to take over and share your comfort with her." Then I thought of a devotional book I had in my own carry-on case. As I pushed the drink cart down the aisle, I handed her the book and opened it to a couple of readings I hoped could encourage her. "I'm sorry," I said. "All I can offer you right now are these words. I hope they can provide some comfort for you." She thanked me, and I went on with my work. A couple of times during the flight, I stopped to ask how she was doing or just to pat her shoulder. When we landed in Atlanta I went in and delivered her to a gate agent to help her make connections before I rejoined my crew for our next flight. I never expected to see or hear from the woman again.

A few weeks later my supervisor called me in to show me a letter. This lady had written Republic to thank the airline for the love and compassion I'd shown her in the midst of her shock and grief. She said I'd been "just the most wonderful friend . . . just like having a member of the family with me." She went on to say "I just can't tell you how wonderful she was to me. You have a super employee and a person who has passengers in mind."

I have to admit I felt pride to have that letter and a commendation from my superiors to go in my file. But I was humbled to realize that when I'd asked God to take over, he had used me as a funnel for his concern to reach this woman in her need.

With positive flying experiences piling up, and what little anxiety that remained slowly shrinking away, I soon realized I was back for good. By the end of the summer, I figured the long pilgrimage that began that stormy afternoon aboard Southern Flight 242 had come to an end.

But a number of significant events still lay ahead.

The first occurred on September 26, 1981, on a flight out to Jacksonville, Florida. Among the passengers boarding the plane in Atlanta was an older couple. The man looked vaguely familiar, but I didn't remember ever seeing his wife—a beautifully dressed woman with a striking air of dignity. I tried to recall where I'd seen the man, but the memory circuits didn't connect. So I went about my regular last-minute chores before takeoff.

It was during the flight, while serving the snack, that I passed the couple and thought, "That man looks like Henry Byrd!" The mere thought of that name made my blood run cold. Henry Byrd had been the president of Southern Airways—the man whose terse note to Mike in Denver had said Southern had done everything they were going to do for me and he saw nothing to be gained in debating the issue further. That letter had symbolized for me Southern's insensitivity and lack of concern for my well-being. In my mind, the name Henry Byrd stood for Southern Airways, and I'd hated them *both*. Now here was this unassuming, aging man who looked like what I remembered about Henry Byrd from the time or two I'd seen him. "But it can't be," I told myself. I passed on down the aisle without saying anything.

But when we landed in Jacksonville and I stood at the door bidding the passengers goodbye, my curiosity got the better of me. As the man and his wife approached, I said, "Sir, you look very familiar to me." Immediately I felt terribly foolish.

He smiled and said, "My name is Henry Byrd."

And I looked him right in the eye and said, "Mr. Byrd, I'm Sandy Purl."

He turned slowly, and embraced me with both arms. Then he stepped back, and with his hands still clasping my shoulders, he beamed into my face and said, "I'm so glad to see you! You're looking wonderful, Sandy. I'm so glad you're back!"

We didn't say anything else, other passengers were still waiting to leave the plane. As I smiled and greeted the final stragglers, I watched Henry Byrd slowly moving on toward the terminal with his wife.

A few minutes later, after a final check of the cabin, I went into the terminal. When I reached the gate, I saw Mrs. Byrd talking on a pay phone and Mr. Byrd sitting and waiting for her. So I walked over and we talked for a while. I told him I'd been back flying almost six months now. He told me he'd retired after the merger, and he and his wife were building a condo in Jacksonville to be near their grandchildren. We chatted some about other Southern Airways people we both knew. Then his wife came, and it was time for them to go.

Before he left, Mr. Byrd gave me another warm embrace. I walked with them to the escalator heading down to the lower level and waved goodbye. And perhaps it was my imagination, but as I watched Henry Byrd moving slowly away down that escalator, he seemed to stand a little taller, a little straighter than he had when he'd gotten on the plane a short while before.

I know the cleansing tears coursing down my face as I watched him go were not only in my imagination. Neither was my thought as that kindly man disappeared in the crowd. "You'll never know this, Mr. Byrd," I thought. "But I forgive you." In that same instant I also forgave Southern Airways. Suddenly I felt a reservoir of pent-up bitterness flow out of me and a sweet sensation of forgiveness wash in and over me—as if someone had taken a pitcher of soothing, warm water and poured it slowly over my head. I thanked God for his healing forgiveness and the new perspective it gave me.

Chapter 20

A little more than six months after my return to the line, I was working a flight from Memphis to Huntsville. I always enjoyed flying with the crew I worked with that month. I got along great with the two women flying with me. The captain, Jimmy Hunt, had always been one of my favorites, too. He'd growl and grouse at me, and I'd dish it right back. He was known as a big joker, but he could take it as well. Once I sewed the sleeves of his flight jacket together; on other occasions, I'd planted surprises in his suitcase. One time he wore his hat half a day before he realized I'd pinned his wings on upside down.

I worked the senior position in the front of the plane on that trip. But during the flight I took one walk back through the cabin. As I did, the passenger in the B seat three rows from the back of the plane smiled and asked, "How are you?"

So I stopped and said, "I'm fine, thanks. You've been on a flight with me before, haven't you?"

I tried to place him as he smiled and replied, "I sure have. You're Sandy, aren't you?"

"Whoops," I thought, "I must have spilled coffee on this guy once or something." But I asked, "Who are you?"

"I'm Don Foster."

Two seconds later we were in each other's arms embracing. Don Foster had been one of my passengers on Flight 242. I hadn't seen him since the NTSB hearings two months after the crash when he testified how he'd moved to an aisle seat just before impact (the exact same seat he now sat in). When the plane finally came to rest, he had pulled his jacket over his head and run out through the flames, sustaining burns to his hands and his head and the temporary loss of all his hair.

I finally let go of Don, telling him I wanted to come back and talk as soon as I finished serving. When I got back to the galley, I

176

did what I always do in emotional times—I cried. But these were happy tears that came with the overwhelming realization of what we'd shared and how far we'd come. Here we were together again on an airplane. He was my passenger once again. Naturally, the two other flight attendants wanted to know what was going on. When I told them who Don was and tried to explain my feelings, they cried, too.

I'm sure the other passengers must have figured we were old boyfriend and girlfriend when I sat down beside Don for the last few minutes of the flight. We talked like a couple of old friends, bringing each other up to date on where we were living and what we'd been doing. I know each of us had our own private thoughts and memories as we talked, but I think we both felt an unexplainable bond and a profound gratitude at the thought I'm certain we both shared: "Just think of everything that's happened to bring us safely together again."

When we reached Huntsville, Don was one of the first passengers off the plane. I watched as he descended the steps from the plane. As he stepped off that last step onto the pavement, a surprising, sudden tidal wave of relief swept through me: "This time I got you down safely."

I watched Don walk to the terminal, where he turned and waved goodbye. Then I ducked into the cockpit where the other passengers wouldn't see me crying. The other flight attendants had already told the cockpit crew what was going on. So I knew I didn't need to explain, but I did say, "I'm sorry. But I'm just going to have to cry for a couple more minutes."

Without looking up, the captain reached back and gave my hand a gentle squeeze. He gazed out the window toward the terminal door, but I still could see the tears trickling down his tanned face as he said, "That's okay, Sandy. Sometimes some of us just have to do that."

Tears rolled down my cheeks long after the plane emptied. But on our final leg of the journey, I served my passengers and fulfilled my duties easily; my job was second nature again. In my mind I replayed the moment when Don disembarked. I saw him step off of the metal stairs and walk toward the terminal across the concrete runway.

"He's safe. I got him down safely this time." The warm congratulations I felt showed in a quiet smile on my face. For the first time in a long time I didn't try to stop the memory from replaying and replaying a scene from the past.

When we landed I bid goodbye to my passengers as they walked off the plane. None knew what was happening inside of me. A chapter in my life had come to an end after paragraphs and paragraphs of pain. Don was safely on his way home. I was confident and secure in my job and self.

Just as the grass and foliage in New Hope had grown up amid the wreckage and covered the crash site from view, time and God's touch had closed the gaping wounds in my soul. Southern Flight 242 was over.

Epilogue

I've been back to flying full time for more than five years. As each year passes I am more and more appreciative of my new life. The experiences, lessons, and opportunities that followed the crash are now all a part of me, and the job I continue to love and enjoy.

One sequence of events in 1982 served to convince me that I, Sandy Purl, have the chance to offer a gift to others simply because I am a survivor.

In January of that year, I had a day off and made lunch plans with a friend. Atlanta was blanketed with its first, and probably only, major snow of the year. After eating we bundled up and walked to Piedmont Park, a couple of blocks from my condominium. I wanted to lie on the ground and make snow angels as I had done when I was a kid. When we returned, laughing and cold, to my home to warm up with hot chocolate, I turned on the T.V. A news bulletin pre-empted the regular program: an Air Florida plane had crashed in Washington, D.C. Details were sketchy, but the report said the plane had plunged into the Potomac on takeoff from Washington National Airport.

I was still glued to the television screen a short while later when the Atlanta station began showing the remarkable video-cam footage of the rescue helicopter plucking survivors from the frozen river. As the chopper maneuvered above the wreckage and lifted a young woman high above the ice and swung toward the safety of shore, I saw her serving apron whipping in the breeze. And I collapsed to my knees in front of the TV exclaiming, "Oh, God. That's a flight attendant."

For the next few minutes I prayed for that girl, asking God to give her the strength she was going to need to put her life back together in the difficult months and years I knew were sure to come. It wasn't until later that night when I learned that the young woman's name was Kelly Duncan. Then I prayed for her by name.

Three days later I worked a flight into Miami, the home base of Air Florida. I walked into the crew lounge and asked to speak with the flight attendant supervisor. I introduced myself as a Republic flight attendant and told her I just wanted to offer my own and Republic's sympathy in Air Florida's time of grief and loss. After she thanked me, I explained that I'd survived a fatal crash and I knew Kelly and the other survivors were going to be experiencing a number of common reactions. I explained briefly about Del Mott and Margaret Barbeau's research because I wanted her to know there were resources available for understanding and preparing for the emotions of survivors. She thanked me for my interest and my concern, and I told her to feel free to contact me if there was anything I could do.

In the weeks and months that followed, I sent Kelly Duncan three get-well cards and two letters. A couple of times I called her mother, who lived near Atlanta, to express my concern and tell her a little bit about what common reactions to expect. Kelly's mom, Mrs. Kleinschmidt, told me she and Kelly both remembered my crash, and she thanked me for my concern.

Then came the day, during the spring of 1983, when I scheduled a pass ride on an Air Florida flight to San Salvador. I took my seat on the very last row of the plane, just in front of the galley. A woman in uniform stuck her head around the corner of the galley to say something to one of the other crew members and my heart began a drum solo in my chest. The woman looked like the pictures I'd seen of Kelly Duncan, but the hair was different—longer. Then she smiled, and I saw the braces. Kelly had braces.

Knowing the crew had a lot to do before takeoff, I didn't ask. But when the woman I thought might be Kelly took her place up in the middle of the cabin for the safety announcements, I asked the attendant closest to me, "Is that Kelly Duncan?"

She nodded. "Yes, it is."

"Would you tell her when she gets a chance I'd like to talk with her a minute?"

"Sure," she replied. After we'd been airborne for a while Kelly walked back the aisle and said, "You wanted to see me?"

I reached up from my seat and put my hand on her arm. "I just knew God would bring us together some day. I just didn't know it would be on an airplane like this." Seeing a puzzled look on her face I added, "I'm Sandy Purl."

"Sandy," she gasped, and we fell into each other's arms. Later, when she'd finished serving her passengers, she sat beside me and talked.

"I don't know what's happening," she said, explaining that in two days she was going in for her very first session with a therapist. "I don't understand. It's been fifteen months since the crash. I thought I was over it. But there are many more long-term memories and fears than I ever imagined."

I was able to assure her all the reactions were normal. "It was eighteen months after my crash before I felt ready for therapy."

We talked together until the end of the flight. When I deplaned in San Salvador, we both knew it had been God's timing that we finally met on that plane on that day.

Ever since the day that I met Kelly, I've continued to work within the airline industry to broaden understanding and inform people of the help available to those who survive an air disaster. I'm often asked to tell the story of Flight 242 to civilian and military safety groups, emergency disaster teams, and people such as crash investigators. Each time, I pray that I have served to increase the listeners' level of sensitivity to survivors and prepared them to face any reaction they might face if ever exposed to a disaster trauma.

In the winter of 1985, I attended a week-long training program in Palm Springs with 450 other airline employees representing fifty-five carriers from around the world. The cabin safety symposium gave ample opportunity for people to tell their stories of survival. This time I didn't tell of my experience; I listened to others describe their reactions and memories both during and after their crises. I thought to myself, "All of these people are hearing firsthand what happens to a survivor. The sensitivity level has certainly come a long way in the industry in the last few years." I felt so grateful. That progress gives me great hope for more change in the future.

The airline industry, as far as it has come, still needs wider exposure to the problems of those who survive an industry disaster. Unions, management and employees remain unaware of and fail to use the research, case studies, and psychological help available. To date, there is no formal prescribed program in any contract or official company policy to provide immediate, ongoing, and comprehensive support—emotionally, financially, and professionally—in the aftermath of a crash.

Besides emphasizing to me the importance of advocating for the rights of survivors, that Air Florida flight, on which I met Kelly, had another significance. I'd arranged for the flight so that I could deliver medicine to a Salvadorean orphanage and pick up a child to deliver for Children's Services International. Like a number of nonprofit international adoption agencies around the country, CSI uses airline personnel and their free pass privileges to help keep the delivery costs down. I've made a number of trips now to places such as Colombia, El Salvador, and Korea. Each time I step off a plane with a little child in my arms ready to place the little orphan in the eager arms of its adoptive parents, I poignantly remember walking away from another airplane dragging a dead body under each arm. To be able to cradle new life and celebrate in the happiness that awaits the children is something I have to thank God for repeatedly. My job once brought sadness to my life. Now it allows me great joy—and hope for continual new life.

I'm also remarried. Bob, a Republic pilot, is a wonderfully supportive man who listens to the memories I sometimes have to share. He patiently comforts me when a nightmare wakes me. But the nightmares, like the memories, aren't so frequent anymore. I spend much more time today dreaming about the future than I do reliving the past.

Like the nightmares, the fear is almost gone. Flying is routine once again. Well, it is on most days.

One last mid-air encounter proved the exception. On February 6, 1984, our flight out of Atlanta bound for Nashville and Chicago carried only nineteen passengers. With three flight attendants and one snack to serve in 45 minutes of flying time, we didn't have a lot to do. When we went into a holding pattern over Nashville, waiting for a snowstorm and fog to clear, I sat down in seat 2C to talk to a friendly lady riding Business Class. One of the flight attendants, Linda, sat directly in front of me in 1C, and the third girl, Nancy, joined our conversation leaning on the armrest directly across the aisle from me at 2B. And there we chatted, waiting for the captain's announcement about whether we'd land, go on to the next stop, or head back to Atlanta.

Suddenly with no warning whatsoever, a lightning bolt, sounding like an iron cannonball on impact, struck the plane just to the left of the plane's nose. In a single bound Nancy leaped from across the aisle from me into Seat 3C directly behind me. That same instant a ball of fire entered through the shell of the plane where the lightning struck, passed the full length of the cabin, and exited through the tail, leaving a heavy acrid smell. I felt the plane begin to drop and my first thought was "Oh please God, not again."

I'd heard a number of passengers cry out, and Nancy muttered, "I was really a cool one, wasn't I?" And I knew, since the entire crew had been in full view of all the passengers, everyone had seen our reactions.

"Stay in your seats and buckle up," I ordered the other two cabin crew members as I leaped to my feet. I raced to the PA mike. "Ladies and gentlemen, we have just experienced a bolt of lightning. There is nothing to be afraid of. I'm sure the captain will be briefing us shortly. In the meantime, check your seatbelts and make sure they are securely fastened."

Thinking "I need to be visible to reassure the passengers," I walked all the way back through the cabin, offering a reassuring pat on the shoulder here, an encouraging smile there. The entire time, I tried to smell for any hint of an electrical fire. But I smelled nothing.

In the cockpit, the pilot and copilot hurriedly assessed the damage. The DC-9 had lost the autopilot, the reverse thrust, and the antiskid. The lightning had also screwed up the compass. But a few minutes later a hole opened in the fog and the pilots set their crippled bird down right in the center of Nashville's main runway.

After a short taxi, the plane pulled to a halt at the terminal and nineteen shaken passengers deplaned.

One of the flight attendants said, "You were terrific, Sandy."

A few moments later I walked through the door into Nashville Operations to see a number of veteran Southern employees on duty. "Is there a phone I could use?" I asked.

"Sure, Sandy," one of the guys responded. "In here." And he guided me into an empty office. But as I walked behind the desk to sit down, every muscle in my body seemed to twitch and my teeth started clattering in my jaws.

"Are you okay, Sandy?"

I started to explain about the lightning, but all that would come out was "Th-th-th-th-th-th."

My trusty tear ducts turned on again and my next thought was a panicky, "I can't let the rest of the crew see me like this!"

Simultaneously, the captain, a man I'd only flown with once before, stuck his head around the corner and looked in the office. When he saw my ashen face, he stepped in and said, "You just go ahead and let it out. Go ahead and be scared. We were all scared. But you were wonderful. After what you did today, I'd fly with you anywhere, Sandy Purl."

One of the operations men asked if he could get me a drink of water and rushed off as soon as I nodded. A few minutes later, my shakes and tears subsided.

During the ten-hour delay before the flight was finally canceled and we ferried the repaired airplane back to Atlanta, the Nashville team responded supportively, checking with each of us in the crew to make sure we felt all right and didn't need anything. When I thanked one of them for their special compassion and care, he just shook his head. "I may not have been up there, " he replied. "But I saw the faces of those passengers get off that plane. And I know you earned your pay today."

Nearly a year later, during a short time of heavy turbulence, sitting in the rear jump seat of a Republic DC-9, I caught myself thinking, collected and calmly, *"Now, what would I do if this plane* crashed? I'd either go forward to those windows, or I'd open the back door. I don't think I'd take four years to start flying again."

Comparatively few people have walked away from an airplane crash. Nonetheless, I recognize that thousands upon thousands of people have suffered their own life-shattering traumas in accidents of varying kinds, natural tragedies, and victimizing acts of violence.

To all survivors I have one bit of encouragement, for I know after every disaster there is an aftermath. Long after the headlines are history, the hurt and healing continue. The few others who have known similar circumstances can understand. Let them help. Don't ignore or deny your pain. Professional counseling helps to reassure that one's feelings are understandable and real. And most of all God offers strength beyond all possible comprehension. The One who saved me from the tragedy of my life and brought me through the aftermath makes me supremely grateful that I am alive.